To Kevin
My friend and fellow
with all best wish... Graham

Conspiracy of Faith

See you on the 'Out'!

Fighting for Justice
after Child Abuse

Graham Wilmer

Ⓛ

The Lutterworth Press

The Lutterworth Press
P.O. Box 60
Cambridge
CB1 2NT

www.lutterworth.com
publishing@lutterworth.com

First Published in 2007

1 3 5 7 9 8 6 4 2

ISBN: 978 0 7188 3058 8

British Library Cataloguing in Publication Data
A catalogue record is available from the British Library

Printed in the United Kingdom by
Bath Press

Contents

For Martin

**In a world of hurt, you stood by me
and gave me the strength to survive.
Thank you my friend.**

Chapter 1

Blind Faith

It was cold and dark outside. Christmas was just three weeks away. As I sat in my study, tidying up the papers I had been working on all day, my fax machine, hidden under a pile of documents, burst into life. I cleared a path through the heap of news cuttings, letters and reports to allow its message the freedom it demanded. The ivory paper began to snake its way across the desk and onto the floor, forming neat waves on the carpet where it fell. When it was done, I collected up the folded epistle and tore it from the machine.

'Case Summary for the Salesian Province of Great Britain', proclaimed the cover page. So, finally, here it was. The document I had been waiting for that I had thought would enable me to complete my journey of recovery was in my hands at last. It was dated 3 December, 2000. I began to read it but, the more I read, the more I knew I was not looking at salvation, I was looking instead into the eyes of despair itself – and it was looking back at me, and smirking. My journey was far from over – let me explain.

On the morning of 6 September, 1963, I was one of 36 boys standing proudly in our new purple blazers and caps at the gates of the Salesian College in Chertsey, Surrey. It was the first day of term in my new school. I was nearly 12 years old, eager, keen and excited at the prospect of meeting new friends and learning new things. A bell began to ring and we filed into the school, across the playground and through a large wooden door that led to our classroom.

Our housemaster – a dowdy old priest, who smelt of BO and tobacco – showed us to our desks. The shoulders of his faded black cassock had a heavy dusting of dandruff on them that made him look a little like a cake decoration. He introduced himself and began to call out our names, each boy answering 'yes father' when it was our turn. We were ordered to sit down and be silent, but not all of us were. The punishment was swift and violent. With the stealth of a lion, the old priest moved quickly from the front of the class to the back, where I was sitting, and struck me across the face with his open hand. I had not even seen him coming, such was my excitement at discovering the books, pencils, erasers, rulers and bits of crisp in my desk, left by the previous occupant.

The blow left me stunned for a few seconds until I realised what had happened. I looked at the priest, who stared back at me with a fierce expression that filled me with dread.

'When I say silent boy – I mean silent. Do you understand me?'

'Yes father.'

'Yes father – what?'

'Yes father – sorry father.'

'Sorry eh? You will be boy – you will be.'

The rest of the class was so quiet you could have heard a pin drop as the old priest shuffled back to the desk at the front of the class and sat down. The boy sitting next to me looked at me with sympathy and smiled. Martin was to become one of my closest friends, but neither of us could have imagined the tragic events that lay ahead of us; nor could we have known the loving bond that would develop between us, cementing our friendship for all time.

By the end of the first term, I had settled into the routine of the school and learnt how to avoid the worst of the punishments that the priests handed out with relish and regularity to any boy who failed to follow the strict rules of the Salesian teaching method, which were basic – do what we tell you or you get beaten. By now, I had also formed good friendships with three of the boys in my class, Martin, Michael and Paul. We sat next to each other in class, spent the break times together and travelled part of the way home together on the train from Chertsey to Weybridge, where Paul lived, and where the rest of us changed trains – Martin going on to New Malden, while Michael and I went south to Byfleet. These were such happy times, filled with laughter, teasing, jokes and girls – lots of them – from a Roman Catholic girls' school and a large comprehensive school, both in Chertsey.

The four of us competed against each other in class, always trying to get the highest marks in end of term exams. Martin and I also fought each other in Archery. We were both average at football and cricket, but unmatched in archery. Between us, we saw off just about everyone else in endless competitions, some, but not all of which, I won by a narrow margin. Martin would often snatch victory from me with his last arrow, which would miraculously finds its way to the very centre of the target, much to the delight of the other boys – who always wagered pocket money or snacks from the tuck shop on the outcome!

As the months came and went, the friendships between the four of us grew stronger, as we got to know and understand each other better. We also shared another bond – our Roman Catholic faith. Having been baptised, we had all been under varying degrees of religious influence from our parents, but none of us realised the power of the daily brainwashing being fed to us in parallel to the curricular education we were receiving from the Salesian priests, shaping the direction of our thinking to suit their own beliefs.

Most of what we did – we were told repeatedly by the priests – was sinful. Lesser sins, such as thinking about girls, telling lies, and disobeying our parents, were dealt with relatively lightly, but the more serious sins, such as missing mass on Sundays, taking Holy Communion without first having gone to confession, and, worst of all, masturbating, were among a long list of 'mortal sins'. These, we were told, would mean we would burn for eternity in the fires of hell if we died without having been granted absolution by a Roman Catholic priest. We found such threats very real at the time, and our development into adolescence was fundamentally twisted by these ridiculous rules – rules made by celibate men who seemed neither to care about, nor understood, the damage they were doing to our young minds.

Harmful though this was, it paled into insignificance compared with the consequences of talking in class, not completing homework on time, or any other transgression, regardless of its seriousness, of school rules, all of which were punished by beatings of one form or another, by hand, fist, belt or cane.

In the absence of anything else, however, you accept what is in front of you, so we carried on in our blind faith – worthless sinners, seemingly unable to find the purity of thought demanded of us – unaware that it was natural, normal and a vital part of the human condition for males to think about the opposite sex for most of the time!

Towards the end of the second year, Martin invited me to spend time at his home in New Malden. His parents were very friendly towards me, and I seemed to blend into his family quite well from the moment I met them. His father was a surgeon at Kingston Hospital. He had a great sense of humour and there was always much laughter ringing around the house. His mother was a kind woman, full of warmth and generosity. She was also a fabulous cook, so mealtimes at the house were always something to look forward to with relish, very unlike the lumpy, cold mashed potatoes and gristly mince we were fed at school.

But food was not the only thing of wonder in that house. Martin had three sisters and a brother, all older than him, and all sharing the same sense of fun and mischief that radiated round the house. The youngest of the three girls, Nicky, was eleven months older than Martin. I did not meet her the first time I went to stay there, but I heard a lot about her and saw photos of her. She was very pretty and it was obvious that she was very dearly loved. When I finally met her, some weeks later, I was completely mesmerised. She was far more beautiful in real life than her photos had been able to show– her smile, her laugh, her walk, her warmth. She was the most wonderful thing I had ever known.

The first time you fall in love is so different to any other experience you will ever have. The waves of stomach churning butterflies, the bursts of rapid pulse rate, the hot flushes, the sleeplessness, the inability to eat – and it goes on and on for weeks. You think it will never stop – and then, if you are very, very lucky, you discover to your total amazement that the person you can't get out of your mind feels the same way about you.

It was at the beginning of the summer holiday, 1966. I had met Nicky on several occasions now, but I had not yet plucked up the courage to tell her how I felt about her. I had told Martin, however. What I did not know was that he had told her! On this visit to their house, I had only been there a short while when Martin asked me to come into the dining room with him, and without saying anything more, he led me into the room. Nicky was standing at the far end of the long, oak table. She was smiling. Martin turned and left the room, closing the door on the way out. Nicky walked across the room to where I stood, pulled me slowly towards her and kissed me gently on the lips. It was like being hit by a train. Could this really be happening? I put my arms around her and kissed her gently on her neck. She was wearing a wonderful perfume that filled my senses to the point of dizziness. I kissed her again and again. My heart was exploding. It really was happening – I was falling in love for the very first time – and miracle of miracles – this beautiful creature was telling me through her kisses that she was fond of me too.

I was in heaven – but there lurked an evil force that was moving slowly in my direction. None of us could have known it was there, but nor could we have done anything to stop it. When it finally arrived, it would destroy me, but for now, there was still a little time left to love and laugh and be happy. The memories of those precious times remain as some of the happiest of my life. They were filled with such innocent tenderness and warmth.

Chapter 2

The Devil's Web

When we returned from the school summer holiday in September 1966, a new teacher had joined the staff. He was tall, young and energetic. Why he chose me is still something I don't fully understand, but, whatever his reasons were, I was the one. It took a while for him to worm his way into my life, but so skilful was he that by the time he was ready to pounce, I was so firmly caught in his web that there was no possibility of escape.

He is Hubert Cecil Madley – though he hated his first name and insisted that I call him Hugh. He began weaving his web by offering to take me home on the back of his motorcycle – a large 600cc Matchless. The rides became frequent, and they served more than one purpose. It gave him the time to befriend me, while at the same time splitting me away from my friends. I spent more and more time with him and less and less with my friends who began to grow slightly cold with me. Before long, he had persuaded my parents to let him give me extra maths lessons at my house.

Madley also had a car, a custard yellow Ford Anglia. One afternoon, at the end of school, he offered to take me home in the car. The journey took about twenty minutes, during which time he said very little to me. I felt that something was not right, but I had no idea what it was. There was a definite sense of unease in the car as we made our way along the Old Woking Road that led to the estate in Pyrford where I lived with my parents and my three sisters, one older and two younger. My dad was an aircraft designer. He was a very private man with a close circle of friends, all based within his world of aeroplanes, a world that consumed him and them, keeping him distant from my sisters and me. My mum was a beautiful woman, charming, but quite shy. She came from a background where wives did what they were told. She was very kind and showered us all with love, but she had suffered from a depressive illness since the loss of her second pregnancy, which would have been my elder brother, had he lived, which tormented her for many years.

As the car approached the turning to our estate, Madley put his hand onto my right leg. I tried to remove it, but he resisted and moved it up to my crotch. I was frozen with fear. I simply did not know what to do. For a few moments, he rubbed my crotch, and then removed his hand. Before I could say anything, he began to talk about masturbation. Did I masturbate? He said. I muttered something inaudible. He repeated the question, even though we were now within sight of my house. I wanted to get out of the car even though we were still moving. I opened the door, but he stopped me by holding my arm tightly until the car was stationery. He spoke in a calm voice and told me that it was only a bit of fun.

I got out of the car and ran to the backdoor. My mother was in the kitchen preparing tea. She seemed to look right through me. I went upstairs and sat on my bed. Then I heard Madley's voice again. He was downstairs talking to my mother about my next maths lesson. I heard someone coming up the stairs. My door opened and there he stood, smirking like a Cheshire cat. He came over to my bed and sat down next to me. Without saying a word, he put his hand back on my crotch and started to rub me. As he did so, he said in a clearly threatening tone that I must not tell anyone about this. It was our secret. He stopped touching me, got up and left.

After a while, I went downstairs. He was gone. My mother began to say what a nice man he was. How lucky I was to have such a caring teacher who seemed to have taken such an interest in me. I wanted to say something – but the words simply would not come out. I felt sick and went back to my room. My mother came up to see if I was all right. I told her that I did not feel well and I was going to bed. She muttered something about a stomach bug that was doing the rounds, and left the room. I lay on my bed in a state of complete shock, eventually falling asleep, waking up the next morning still in my school uniform.

When I arrived at school the next day, Madley was waiting for me in the playground. He came up to me and walked me away from my friends on the pretext that he wanted to discuss my maths lessons. When we were far out of earshot he asked me if I had said anything. I said no and he told me that there would be serious consequences if I ever did. I looked at him without speaking. I felt numb.

At the end of school, Madley said he would take me home again. I wanted to go home on the train with my friends, but he insisted, saying that he had agreed with my mother that he would give me another lesson at home that evening. I said farewell to Martin and the others and walked with him to the schoolhouse he lived in halfway down Station Road. His car was parked outside and I went to the passenger door to get in.

'We're not going just yet,' he said. 'I want to show you something.'

I followed him into the hallway. The house was dark and smelt of stale clothes. He opened a door and went in. I remained in the hallway, expecting him to come out again with what ever it was he wanted to show me.

'Come in a moment,' he said. I went into the room – it was cold and smelt musty. Madley was sitting on a single bed. There was a wooden chair by the end of the bed, piled with clothes, and a small table under the window which looked out into the tiny front garden and onto the road. Drab lace curtains hung limply at the window, filtering the light preventing people from looking in.

On the table sat a piece of electronic equipment and a soldering iron. There were drawings and wiring diagrams scattered on the floor. Madley stood up and picked up the piece of equipment.

'Do you know what this is?' he asked.

'Not really – it looks like a radio,' I replied.

'Not quite – it's a signal generator. I have been building it from a kit. I'll show you how it works in a minute. Come here first.'

Madley pulled me over to the bed and sat me down. Without saying anything else, he opened his flies and took out his penis. I was so shocked; I sat there staring at him, saying nothing. He took my right hand and placed in on his penis and began to rub it. It did not take long before he let out a moan and ejaculated. His semen spattered on my face, my blazer and dribbled down my hand. I felt I was going to be sick, but the fear inside me was so intense I stayed motionless. Madley began to laugh. He took out a white hanky from his suit pocket and started to wipe me down. The smell of his semen was the same musty smell I had noticed when I entered the room.

When he had finished cleaning me, he asked me if I had enjoyed it. I just looked at him and said nothing.

'It won't hurt you – it's what men do. It's good for you.'

'Can we go home now please?' I asked.

'O.K., but the same rules apply. You say nothing to anyone about this, understood?'

I agreed and we left the room, got into the car and he drove me home. When we reached the house, instead of coming in, he said goodbye and drove off.

Over the next few weeks, Madley took me to his house almost every day. On the second visit, he took my trousers down and masturbated me before making me do the same to him. At the end of each session, he would repeat his demands that I tell no one, only now he began to add the penalties that would follow.

'No one will believe you.'

'You will be outcast by your friends.'

'You will be told to leave the school.'

The list was long, dire and terrifying. I was totally trapped in his web of secrets and lies. I felt empty, vulnerable and consumed with guilt, but my nightmare had only just begun.

Chapter 3

Love Lost

As the months rolled on, I began to display signs of the depression I was sliding into. My schoolwork deteriorated sharply, I became reclusive and solemn. I lost weight and spent hours alone in my room. My parents thought I was just being a typical moody teenager, but my school reports showed quite clearly that something was wrong. My father began to challenge the headmaster about my poor performance, but the responses he got were dismissive. Over time, these exchanges were to become hostile, but at no time did anyone sit down with me and ask me what was wrong.

Martin's house became a sanctuary for me and I spent as much time there as I could. I said nothing to anyone about what was going on, but Nicky sensed I had changed. I had grown cold and fearful of physical contact. We had only ever kissed, but she was the first girl I had ever kissed, and the kisses we shared had been gentle and sweet – filled with love and excitement. But now I found it almost impossible even to kiss her. I felt so dirty, so violated. I simply could not bear to be close to her in case she discovered somehow that I was no longer the person she thought I was.

I had only known her for six months before the abuse began. Six wonderful months that had turned my life upside down. I tried to hold on to her, but the gulf between us grew wider and wider until, not surprisingly, she told me she had met someone else and didn't want to go out with me any more. Under normal circumstances, I should have been able to cope better with this, but the impact of hearing those words in the state I was in pushed me into a deep despair that totally consumed me.

Some months before, Nicky had given me a lock of her hair in a piece of blue tissue paper. I kept the lock of hair in the left pocket of my school blazer. When Madley abused me, I would slip my left hand into the pocket and touch the tissue paper. It was the only link I had between the horror of what he was doing to me, and something of beauty. It helped me cope with what was happening. I would close my eyes and see her face while he destroyed me. Sometimes, he would insist that I took my clothes off, so I would lay the blazer next to me and touch the sleeve. He never knew how important it was to me. It was my secret – a secret that I never had to share with him.

In the summer of 1967, Madley persuaded my parents to let him take me on a camping holiday in South Wales. He had relatives there and a cottage that belonged to his father. I did not want to go, but I felt so trapped, I could not find a way out. Had I known what was going to happen, I might have run away, but I didn't know. By now I had come to hate him with such intense anger that I spent the entire journey plotting ways to kill him. He, on the other hand, being blissfully unaware of the darkness of my world, chatted endlessly about this and that. That is one of the things I remember most clearly about Madley – he would talk for hours, yet he said nothing. The only thing I learnt from this man was hatred, pure and cold. It would haunt me for many years to come.

When we finally arrived at the cottage – it was cold and dark. The cottage itself was almost derelict.

'We'll sleep in the tent tonight,' he said, and started to unpack the boot of the car. He took out a shotgun, an Aldis lamp and the tent. It took a while to put the tent up and he became angry, throwing thing around and muttering darkly about how much he hated it when things went wrong. Eventually, the tent was up and he threw two sleeping bags inside it, then walked back to the car and picked up the gun and the lamp.

He walked off towards the fields that backed onto the garden and in-structed me to follow. The lamp cut a swath of light through the darkness as he moved from side to side.

'What are you looking for?' I asked.

'Rabbits,' he replied. 'There are usually hundreds of them here.'

The light from the lamp finally rested on a small group of rabbits about one hundred yards from us. Madley told me to hold the lamp on the startled animals while he loaded the gun and took aim. He fired several times and the rabbits scattered. Madley took the lamp off me and gave me the gun to hold for him. He walked to the place where the rabbits had been sitting. There was nothing there. They had all got away safely. He let out a curse and started to stamp the ground like a petulant child. I had the gun in my hand, but there was no way I could have used it – I was just too scared.

Madley came back across the field scowling. He went into the tent and zipped the two sleeping bags together to form a double one. I had a bad feeling inside my stomach as I watched him.

'Put the gun back in the car, but bring the lamp here,' he snapped. I can't remember a time when he ever said thank you for anything I did, such was the power he had over me. I did as I was told and climbed into the tent. It was not very big, but there was just enough room for me to lie flat without my feet sticking out of the far end. It was then that I noticed there was no ground sheet.

'Won't we get wet?' I asked.

'So what,' said Madley. 'It won't kill you.'

'But I have not brought any spare clothes,' I said.

'Well, tough! You should have thought of that before,' he snapped.

I climbed into the sleeping bag and awaited my fate. Madley struggled in and put his arms round me. I wanted to be sick, but there was nothing I could do. If I resisted, he might get violent. I was on my own. I would just have to go along with it yet again. Once it was done, I would be able to go to sleep. He began to fondle me, and the now familiar course of events unfolded. When he was done, I turned over and tried to go to sleep. It was very cold though and the ground underneath me was damp. I began to shiver and I suggested that we go into the cottage and light the fire in the kitchen.

Madley grudgingly agreed and we moved into the kitchen with the sleeping bags still zipped together.

'I'll get the seats from the car,' he said. 'We can sleep on those.'

I collected some sticks from the wood store at the rear of the kitchen and placed them in the grate of the old range. Madley came back with the car seats from the rear of the car and placed them on the floor. He threw me a box of matches and I found some old newspaper. The wood was so dry that the fire was soon burning well. Its heat gave me a degree of comfort, but that would not last long.

Madley told me to take off my trousers and lie face down on the car seat. He removed all of his clothes, seemingly oblivious to the cold. He had a mad look in his eyes and seemed very agitated. He lay down on top of me and I felt him fumbling around with my bottom. After a few moments, he began to push his penis into my anus. I told him that he was hurting me, but he only paused briefly to spit on my anus. Then he began again, penetrating me for the first time. The combination of pain and fear made me draw a sharp intake of breath, but it was soon over. He ejaculated inside me after only a few seconds and then just lay there uttering a sort of whimpering noise.

When he had finished, he got off, pulled me up by the arm, lay on the seat himself and said 'You do it to me now.'

He took hold of my penis and pushed it between his buttock cheeks. It would not go in. I said that I didn't want to do it. To my surprise he said that was O.K. He turned over and told me to kneel. He then masturbated me, smearing my semen over his chest as I ejaculated. I looked towards the fire. It was still burning well, and, to this day, I can still feel its heat on my face, and the terror I felt in my heart at what had just happened. I wanted to be dead. I lay on the car seat, pulled the sleeping bag over me and tried to sleep. It was a long time before dawn came.

Chapter 4

God's Will

Empowered by his now total control over me, Madley continued to abuse me as often as he could; at my house, at school, in his room – anywhere he could get access to me away from others. It seemed to go on forever, and I can still feel the complete sense of hopelessness I lived with, day in, day out, as if it were yesterday. I could not see any way out of my nightmare, a dilemma he continued to enforce with his daily warnings of the dire consequences I would face if I ever breathed a word of what was happening.

I had long since stopped taking communion at mass as I was clearly in a state of mortal sin, and I could not go to confession and tell the priest what I had done. We had all been told many times that the rules were the rules – you don't mess with the Church, and you certainly don't mess with the Almighty. These sins were just so terrible that I knew I would never be able to confess them and get away with it. I was doomed; I knew it and I believed God knew it. But then that was the way I saw it – the view of a child. God, as I was about to learn, had other plans.

On a cold Saturday morning in February 1968, the Fifth-Form rugby team assembled for a game against a visiting school team. Martin had been selected to play in the team but I had not and was at home, unaware of what happened during the game. It was not until Monday morning that I heard the rumours spreading in the playground about an accident involving Martin. We were not told any details, but I learnt later in the day that he had gone down during a scrum and been fallen on heavily. He did not get up immediately when the scrum dispersed, but when he did, he was dragging his right leg as he walked. Although dazed and limping, Martin attempted to rejoin the game, but was ordered off the field by the coach, Fr Tyler. The seriousness of his injury was not appreciated until he collapsed into unconsciousness, but even then, it was thought he had only suffered concussion. Eventually, an ambulance was called, but it was some twenty minutes before he was taken to St Peter's Hospital in Chertsey, where doctors quickly discovered he had suffered a major internal head injury. Martin was then rushed to Atkinson Morley Hospital, where frantic efforts were made to try and save him. On the Tuesday morning, during assembly, we were told the terrible news that they had lost the battle and he had died the previous day, his parents by his bedside. For the next two days, I was in complete shock, unable even to cry. A terrible atmosphere hung around the playground and the normal ribbing and name calling that we were all used to had fallen silent. None of us knew quite what to say to each other. On the evening of the third day, Martin's father telephoned our house and asked to speak to me. His voice was gentle and calm and I told him how sorry I was. He thanked me and asked me if I would be willing serve as an altar boy at Martin's requiem mass. He said there would be only be two altar boys –Martin's older brother, Paul, and I. The priest taking the mass would be none other than Bishop Wheeler himself, a close family friend of the Allens. I had met him on several occasions at their home and he certainly knew who I was. I told Dr Allen that it would be an honour and I would try not to let him down. He thanked me and said it was what the whole family wanted. I put the receiver back onto its cradle and began to cry.

As I thought about what was to come, I realised that I was now faced with a real dilemma. Ever since the abuse began, I believed that I had fallen from grace. I was in a state of mortal sin and could therefore not take Holy Communion unless I had first been to confession and confessed my awful sins. But how could I possibly go to confession and tell the priest, who also knew me well, that I had committed all these terrible homosexual acts? He would ask questions – it would all come out. The world around me would collapse. All hope would be lost and I would be an outcast.

On the other hand, how could I refuse to take communion from the Bishop at the requiem mass? You see, in the Roman Catholic mass, after the priest has consecrated the host he communicates himself, then the altar boys, and then the members of the congregation. When the Bishop offered me the consecrated host, all eyes would be upon me. How was I going to avoid taking communion? I couldn't avoid it. It would be unthinkable. Martin's family would be heartbroken to see me refuse communion at such an important event in their family life. What was I to do?

With the funeral now only two days away, I finally made up my mind that I would go to confession and face whatever the consequences were to be. It was, after all, 'my fault' that I had committed these terrible sins, so I deserved the punishment that was due. The following day, at break time, I made my way across the playground to the main school building and knocked on the priests' staff room door. The priest who opened it was my housemaster, Fr Madden.

'Can I see you a moment please, Father?' I said.

'Yes, boy, come in.' There was no one else in the room so I came straight out with it.

'I need to confess my sins, Father. Will you hear my confession now please?' The priest was clearly annoyed and began to scowl at me.

'Can it not wait until later?'

'No, Father. It must be now.'

'Very well, follow me.' He led me down the corridor and opened a large, oak panelled door into the priests' private chapel. There was no confessional box in the chapel so he pulled up a kneeling stool and a chair. He gestured to me to kneel on the stool. As I did, he walked over to a large wooden chest of drawers and took out a long, purple stole, which he kissed and placed around his neck like a scarf. He walked back, sat down on the chair next to me and made the sign of the cross.

It was now or never. I made the sign of the cross and began.

'Bless me, Father, for I have sinned. It is several months since my last confession. Father, I have had impure thoughts and done impure things.'

'What sort of things?' he asked.

I murmured in a low voice, unable to say it out loud. The words just did not want to come out of my mouth.

'Speak up, boy! What sort of things?'

'Homosexual acts, Father.' There was a brief pause and he repeated my words.

'Homosexual acts? What kind of acts, boy?'

I started to go through the litany of evil, dirty, disgusting, unspeakable things that I had done with Madley. Fr Madden interrupted me:

'Who did you do all this with, boy?'

This was the moment. The end had arrived. I said Madley's name out loud and waited.

'Do you mean Mr Madley, your science teacher?'

'Yes Father – Hugh Madley.' There was a further pause.

'Have you told me everything about this?'

'No, Father, there is more.' Explaining the acts of buggery was more difficult than I had thought it would be, as I was not really quite sure which part of it was my sin. There was a longer pause when I had finished. Fr

Madden began to tell me that these were very serious matters indeed, as if I didn't already know that. He went on, but in a more caring tone than he had used earlier. He said he wanted me to think about the wider issues that would result from what I had done with Madley. I didn't understand what he meant and I said so.

'The point is, boy, I will obviously need to take this further for your own protection, but I can't unless you repeat what you have said to me outside of confession. Will you do that?' Before I could answer, Fr Madden said:

'Look, make your act of contrition and I will give you absolution. You can then tell me again, once the confession is finished.' I was so relieved to hear those precious words – 'I will give you absolution' – I began saying my contrition prayer. Fr Madden spoke the words of the prayers of absolution and told me to say three Our Fathers and three Hail Marys for my penance. It was done. I was saved.

It was not done at all. Far from being saved, I was about to be betrayed by my confessor. With my head still spinning with the relief at having been granted absolution, I repeated the story again. Fr Madden asked no further questions and then placed his right hand on my head and told me to go now and not to worry about it any more. He said he would need to speak to the Headmaster, Fr O'Shea, and that I would probably have to see him as well. I didn't care. The heaviest weight in all the world had just been lifted from my shoulders. I was free, and I would tell Madley what I had done as soon as I could.

As I made my way back across the playground, I saw him bowling a tennis ball to a couple of boys from the second year. He called me over. As I got closer he saw in my face that something was wrong.

'What's up?' he asked.

'I've told them,' I said. 'I had to – for the requiem mass tomorrow. I'm serving on the altar. I had to.' He looked at me for a moment and then smiled.

'They won't believe you. I'll just deny it.' The two boys, unaware of the gravity of our conversation, called to him: 'Come on, sir, bowl the ball.'

'OK,' said Madley, and he returned to the game. I went into to the main school chapel, lit a candle and said my prayers of penance.

The following day, Martin was laid to rest. The solemnity of the requiem mass was matched with the sincerity of the wonderful tributes paid to Martin by his family and friends. When it came to the communion, Paul and I walked together up the three steps to the main altar and bowed our heads. Bishop Wheeler moved towards us with the chalice and gave us each the host. The church was silent, but my soul was singing. I could feel Martin's presence. His happy spirit was still with us. I looked at Paul for a moment, he looked so lost. As I turned and made my way back to my place at the base of the altar, I looked at Nicky sitting in the front row next to her parents and her two older sisters; her face was so sad. I turned round, faced the altar and sobbed quietly. After the mass, I went with the family to Kingston Cemetery, where dear Martin was laid to rest. I could not have known then, but it would be another 37 years before I would return to that spot and stand in front of his grave once more.

A few days later, I was summoned to see the headmaster during morning break. The rector, Fr Gaffney, was also waiting for me, along with another priest I had not seen before. The rector spoke first, introducing the priest as a 'specialist' in these sort of matters who would talk to me alone about what had happened. All three priests looked extremely glum.

The rector and the head then left the room and the interrogation began. The 'specialist' priest wanted to know every aspect of my sexual history – when had I started to masturbate? Had I done anything like this with any other boys? Did I have sexual fantasies about boys? Had I had sexual contact of any kind with any member of my family? The questions came thick and fast. I became very confused and started crying. The priest paused for a while and told me not to get upset. He then left the room for a moment. When he returned, his tone was more friendly and he talked about how the school would deal with things from now on. I was given strict instructions not to talk to anyone about the matter, including my parents. He said they would speak to me again soon, and that I was free to go now and that I should go straight home. What I did not know was that this priest was none other than the Provincial Rector of the Salesian Order in the UK. He was the boss; the head honcho – God.

The next day, Madley did not turn up for our Chemistry lesson. One of the priests who taught the sixth form came in his place, telling us that Madley was 'unavailable this morning', but would be in school later. After lunch, I saw him in the playground. He was sharing a joke with some of the older boys. When they had gone, I went over to him and asked him what had happened. He looked at me for a moment with his cold, dark eyes, then smiled in triumph.

'I denied it,' he said. 'They don't believe you. I told you, no one would believe you.' I was unable to speak and walked slowly away.

Easter came and went and the weeks rolled on towards summer. It was year five – GCE exam year. Although the sexual abuse had stopped, the psychological damage was only just beginning to make its impact felt. By now I had withdrawn so completely that my mother became seriously concerned about me. The school had still not mentioned a word of my confession to my parents, nor had they said anything more about it to me. I began to suffer bouts of intense stomach cramp which our family doctor put down to 'growing pains'. My loss of appetite and subsequent weight loss was put down to pre-exam nerves, 'not uncommon in boys of my age', my mother was told. The doctor prescribed some vitamin pills; my father told me simply to 'buck my bloody ideas up, or there'd be trouble'.

Unbeknown to me at the time, my father had written to the headmaster twelve months previously in, January 1967, to demand to know why my end of term report was so poor. Without exception, each of my teachers had put negative comments about my performance. 'Very disturbing result', 'This result is the product of a lazy approach', 'Not enough interest in class nor effort at home', 'Very capable in the subject, but mind seems elsewhere', 'Careless, capable of much better', 'Still produces results below his capabilities'.

His letter began: 'I am deeply disturbed by my son's appalling end of term report. Its implications for his future are very serious.' The alarm bells should have been ringing very clearly, yet , on 11 January 1967, the head wrote back to my father: 'You say you are deeply disturbed and cannot any longer let this situation go unchanged. The tone of your letter – even on the smaller points – suggests very strong disapproval. I think I can say that the school has done a great deal for your son in the past four years. If you so strongly dislike what is being done now, perhaps you would prefer to find another school for him.'

Over the following two months, my father wrote several more letters, each time receiving a similar reply. It is not hard to imagine then, after I told them in February of 1968 what had been going on, the predicament that they now found themselves in. If they were to tell my parents what I had told them, the war of words between them would quickly erupt into something far more serious. The implications for this private, fee-paying school could not be underestimated. Their decision – to do and say nothing – was unforgivable, but, having made that decision, they were stuck with it. When my father wrote to them again on 7 March 1968, some three weeks after my confession, he said: 'I have studied Graham's term report with the usual mixed feelings. Not one member of your staff has anything encouraging to say regarding his efforts or diligence, and I continue with the impression that he and form 5a spend too much time playing around instead of concentrating on their studies.'

Fr O'Shea replied by return post in his own hand. He said simply: 'Many thanks for your letter of today. Graham has not done too badly in his mock examinations – apart from Mathematics – and he certainly merits the opportunity of sitting for the subjects you suggest. He has a reasonable chance of success in all of them.' This was the very same priest who had known for the previous three weeks all my secrets, had arranged for the 'specialist' priest to interrogate me after my confession, had listened to the debrief after that interrogation, and had read the subsequent report. Betrayal is the only word to describe the actions of this incompetent school head. But he was not done yet. There was worse to come.

Chapter 5

Wilderness

Without Martin, school seemed even lonelier than before. I saw Nicky a few times after his death, but by now she was having fun with her new boyfriend, and there was no way back for me. I had known for months that our relationship was fractured beyond repair, and even thought I still loved her, I knew I could never turn back time. My beautiful Nicky was gone from my life and my heart was broken. The hatred I felt for Madley and the priests had reached a level that was no longer measurable.

It was in this awful state that I sat down in the school hall on 28 July 1968 and began three days of exams, along with the rest of the fifth year. When it was over, we said our farewells and school was finished for the summer holiday. It would be another 36 years before I would see many of them again.

I can still recall vividly the morning in September when my exam results arrived. I was still in bed when my father came into my room and knelt down by the side of my bed. He had a look of sorrow on his face and he spoke in a soft and gentle manner, most unlike the way he normally spoke to me. When he was done, he got up and left the room. What he had told me took a while to sink in, but when it had, I felt no emotion whatsoever. I had failed every single exam but one, Art, and even in that I had only just scraped a pass. Eight years of going to school had come to nothing, and who was to blame? Well, me, of course. I was obviously as stupid and lazy as everyone had said I was. There was no future for me now. It was over. I pulled the covers up over my head and closed my eyes tightly. In my mind, all I could see was Madley's face smirking and sneering at me.

A few days later, my father told me to telephone the headmaster and ask if I could come back to school in September and repeat the fifth year and retake my exams. When I eventually got through to Fr O'Shea, his voice was cold and empty. 'I'm afraid there is no room for you. We already have 36 in the class. I can't make an exception. I'm sorry, but the answer is no.' This was the second time he had betrayed me, but it would not be the last. There would be a third time, but it would be another 30 years before the old cockerel would crow again.

For reasons which I still don't understand, my father would not speak to Fr O'Shea. Instead, he wrote to the Director of Education at Surrey County Council, determined to 'get something done'. If only he had sat down with me and asked me what was really wrong. I'm sure I would have told him; I was so exhausted with it all – the pretence, the lies, the guilt, the pain. But he didn't and so it went on. His letter was polite and to the point, but it included an important clue, if only they had read the letter more carefully.

'Sir, may I bring to your attention a situation that has just developed regarding my son Graham, 16, who has been a student at Salesian College. Consequent upon encouraging 'mock' GCE examinations, and at the discretion and judgement of his headmaster, he was entered for 7 GCE O level examinations in June of this year. For reasons as yet unclear, Graham failed six of them – with the lowest possible grades, and I have recently been advised that the school cannot offer him the opportunity to continue his education and resit his examinations. Graham has effectively been deprived of any hopes of a full education, and is now prevented from continuing his plans for university. This is an unbelievable situation to which I am totally unable to acquiesce. May I respectfully ask you, therefore, to give this matter your personal and urgent attention in order that Graham may continue with his full-time education to A level standard.'

A week later, the Director of Education replied, saying that he had written to the headmaster of another local school to enquire if they could consider me for admission, and if they were able to admit me, my father would hear from the school directly. In due course, the headmaster of the other school replied. He was very sorry, but there was 'no room at the inn.'

My father, by now exasperated, and still blaming me for my poor effort, told me that I must enrol at the local technical college and retake some O levels. By now I had become so isolated from reality that the next 12 months might as well never have happened. I was living from hour to hour, day to day, not involved and not aware of what was going on around me. At the end of the course, I sat just two O level exams, Biology and English, and I failed again. My father, unable to comprehend my apparent stupidity, said I could forget further education. I must find a job and look for somewhere else to live. He did not want me living at home any more.

So began my years in the wilderness. I worked as a window cleaner's assistant, a hospital porter, a van driver's assistant, a shop assistant, a cinema cleaner, a gardener's assistant, and numerous other manual jobs. Being tall, strong, well-mannered and intelligent – despite what my school record of achievement said – it was not difficult to get work of this kind, but I found it very difficult to stay long in any job. I was also easy prey for paedophiles. If I had thought that I was free from the clutches of evil men, I was very, very wrong. But such is the nature of child abuse. The more often you are damaged, the more vulnerable you become, and my first job quickly exposed just how vulnerable I was to further abuse.

Jim, a crude, gruff, Irishman in his fifties, was our local window cleaner. He had worked on our estate for several years. Everyone knew him. He was also an experienced paedophile and had served time in prison for a range of petty crimes. I did not know that then. He was a strong man, despite being only five foot six inches tall. He had boxed as a younger man and bore the familiar facial scars and broken nose of the sport. My mother had told him about my current position and he offered to give me a job with him for five pounds per week. At the time, I was actually very grateful. At least it would get my father off my back.

Things went well for the first two weeks, then one afternoon, we finished work early and he said he would take me for a drink. I was just 17 years old. After several drinks, I felt slightly the worse for wear. I had not eaten anything all day and the alcohol went to my head quickly. He took me outside to the car park at the back of the pub. It was dark by now. I vomited several times and my head spun like a top. He put me into the back of his dirty old Ford Prefect, climbed in after me and raped me before, eventually, taking me home.

Before we reached the house, he stopped the car and told me that if I said anything to anyone, he would hurt me. He might even have to kill me. For the first time in my life I knew the meaning of terrifying fear; it was different from the fear I had felt when Madley had abused me.

For the next three months, Jim used and abused me in every way he could. I thought up all sorts of plans in my mind to kill him each time he abused me, none of which I was capable of carrying out. I was just too scared. The intimidation continued, then, one evening, on the way home from work, he stopped the car on Pyrford Common. It was dark. He began to fondle me, then he grabbed my face and pulled it towards him. He kissed me hard on the lips and then forced his tongue into my mouth. His foul breath made me want to vomit. I pulled my head back but he held on and tried to kiss me again. I jerked my head left then right, then left to try and avoid his continued attempts. He became very angry and began shouting at me. It was the now familiar tirade: 'After everything I've done for you, given you a job, looked after you, driven you around, taken you to pubs. I treat you like my own son and this is how you repay me.' Then he said something that made me realise just how much danger I was really in.

'I've got other boys, you know. They'll do anything for me. I pay them. I think they should teach you a lesson.' The next day I told my mother that I was going to look for another job and if Jim called for me to tell him that I was not at home. She didn't seem particularly bothered, but with four other children in the family to look after, including a two year old, my youngest sister, she had more than enough to cope with without having to worry about me.

I cycled over to the next village and went to see Ray, a friend whose father ran a DIY shop. I asked him if they had any jobs and, to my delight, his dad said that he could do with some help on a part-time basis: 'I can offer you three afternoons a week and Saturdays for which I'll pay you a fiver'. I said that would be brilliant. It was the same money Jim was paying me, but for fewer hours. I couldn't believe it; I was free from another nightmare, or so I thought.

The new job went without a problem for about three weeks. I really enjoyed it, as Ray's parents, both of whom worked in the shop, were always joking and having a laugh with the customers. It was the opposite of the brutal environment I had experienced working for Jim.

Then, one Saturday, Jim walked into the shop.

'I want to see you,' he demanded. 'Outside.' I told him that I couldn't come out now. 'OK, I'll wait 'till you finish,' he said and walked out. Ray's dad looked concerned and asked me if there was a problem. I said no. 'He was my previous boss and I hadn't given him a week's notice before I left. He's just a bit cross with me.'

Ray's dad went out of the shop and looked up the road. Jim was sitting in his car a few yards away. An hour later he was still there.

'I don't like this,' he said. He went to the phone and called someone. I couldn't hear what was being said, but ten minutes later a burly man in a long trench coat came into the shop and took me into the back room. Ray and his dad came with them. The man in the coat introduced himself as a Detective Superintendent. He said he was also a personal friend of Ray's dad. He started to ask me about Jim and what I thought he was up to. At this stage I did not feel that I was in any jeopardy, after all, I hadn't done anything wrong in my new job. Then came the heat.

'You two are planning to rob this place, aren't you? You're here to case the place and he's going to come back and break in. That's it, isn't it, lad?' I protested with incredulity. But the more I protested the more the detective scoffed at me and repeated the question.

After about ten more minutes of questions, I said, 'OK, I'll tell you what's really been going on,' and I did. When I'd finished, he said simply, 'Right, you and I are going to the police station.' I was bundled outside and stuffed into the back of a police car. Jim was nowhere to be seen. The next four or five hours are still etched on my mind with such clarity that I can still recall virtually every moment of it.

Once inside the police station, I was taken up a flight of stairs and directed to one of three chairs next to a desk on the first-floor landing. I sat down and watched as people hurried passed me, some going up the stairs, some going down. After about ten minutes, two men in civilian clothes came up to me and sat down, one on a chair next to me and one on the edge of the desk. The younger of the two was about 25, the other about 40. The younger man introduced himself as a Detective Constable and gave his name. He then introduced his colleague saying that he too was a Detective Constable, and his name was 'Bubbles'. As the word came out, I repeated it, 'Bubbles?'

'Yes,' said the younger man, 'Bubbles.' Their crude attempt to make a cheap homosexual joke at my expense was lost on me. I simply didn't understand.

Over the next 30 minutes, they questioned me in minute detail about what had gone on, or rather what they said I had 'claimed' had gone on between Jim and myself. They made few notes, but many crude comments to each other, all of a sexual nature. I was then escorted up to the next floor and shown into a large room and told to sit on one side of a number of desks that had been placed together to form a table about 20 feet square. Two other men came into the room and my original escorts left.

The interrogation that followed was painful and cruel. They appeared not to have believed a word I said. They mocked me and laughed at me when I tried to describe some of the detail of what had happened. After a while, I became upset and began to cry. After several minutes, one of the detectives said: 'Look, I'm not trying to upset you. I just need to be sure.' I looked at him and asked, 'What do you need to be sure about?'

'All this stuff,' he said. 'All this stuff about what you say he did to you.'

'Why don't you ask him?' I said.

'I think we will,' he said, and left the room. A while later, he returned and said I was free to go but I should report back to the police station at 9 a.m. the following morning. I made my way home in a dazed, bewildered and frightened, dragging my feet with each step. With a heavy heart, I told my mother what had happened. When my father came home, she took him into the front room and spoke to him. I listened in the front hall. I heard him ask her: 'Is he that way inclined?' She said she didn't know. I was devastated.

My father said nothing at all to me that evening. In the morning, he drove me in silence to the police station. I was shown to a small interview room and he was escorted off to see the Chief Superintendent. After what seemed like an eternity, he returned and told me that I was to be examined by the police surgeon. A short, stocky man with silver hair came into the room shortly afterwards holding a small, leather Gladstone bag. He pointed to a green cloth screen in the corner of the room and told me to take off my trousers and underpants. I went behind the screen, took them off and waited. He spoke to my father in a such a quiet tone, almost a whisper, I couldn't hear what they were saying. He stepped behind the screen and told me to bend over. He pushed a wooden spatula into my anus, removed it and put it in a plastic bag. He then put some lubricant cream on his right forefinger and proceeded to examine me internally for about 30 seconds. It didn't really hurt, but it was uncomfortable.

Afterwards, he told me to get dressed and wait in the room. He left the room with my father and I sat and waited. Twenty minutes later, my father, accompanied by the Chief Superintendent came back in. To my astonishment, the Chief Superintendent handed me a piece of paper and said I should sign it, and then I could go. I read the document carefully. It was a retraction for the allegations I had made and an apology for wasting police time. I looked at my father. He too told me to sign it, saying it was in my 'best interests'. I signed it and gave it back to the Chief Superintendent. Apparently, the medical examination had shown no signs of injury, and Jim had, of course, flatly denied the offences when the police had gone round to see him the previous evening. They told my father that they would, however, 'keep an eye on him'.

On the way home my father tried to justify the 'deal' he'd done with the police. I should be very grateful for their understanding and helpful response to this very 'difficult and messy situation'. I thought about his 'deal' for years to come. It may have been a good 'deal' for him, and I can understand why he thought it was the best thing for me. But it was not. For me, it was a tragedy. How could I ever tell anyone about what Madley had done to me? No one would believe me now, not after 'wasting police time'. I would just have to get on with my life and try to forget what had happened. If only it could have been that simple.

I began to see another of my school friends, Paul, on a regular basis. He lived about eight miles away. His parents were absolutely wonderful and they too began to treat me like another son. His sister Liz was also a joy to be with, funny, happy and gorgeous. I shared some of the best times of my teenage years with them. It was safe house, a kind house, a musical house. A sanctuary from all my troubles. I loved them dearly and still do.

Not long after the police incident, I got a job as a sales assistant at Derry and Toms in Kensington, and took a room in a hostel in Notting Hill. I shared the room with two other lads. They were nice enough, but I was desperately lonely. The food was good though and I settled into a routine of sorts, going to work, going back to the hostel, having a meal in the canteen and going to bed. Weekends were the loneliest, as my two room mates both went home for the weekends. I stayed there, not wanting to go home.

As I soon discovered though, a London store was the wrong place for a vulnerable victim of sexual abuse. I was an easy target for the older, more predatory homosexuals who worked there. One of them, a man in his early sixties, worked the lift. Each time I got in it to go to the floor where I worked, he would make sexual remarks to me, even if there were other people in the lift.

As the weeks went by, his remarks became more personal. On one particular morning, I got into the lift, the only passenger. He closed the gates and off we went. Instead of stopping at my floor, the third, he took the lift to the top floor where the staff canteen was. He took hold of my arm and put his hand on my bottom and began to rub it. I pulled away and told him to stop, which he did. My heart was beating fast; I was desperate to get out. He took the lift back to the second floor and opened the gates. I flew out of the lift, and out of the store. I never returned. 'What is it about me?' I kept asking myself.

The next day, I took a bus to St Thomas' Hospital and asked if they had any vacancies for porters. I was in luck and after a short interview with the beadle, I was told to report to the porters' lodge the following Monday. It was the best job in the world. The doctors never spoke much, usually too engrossed in their work, but that was more than made up for by the nurses, hundreds and hundreds of them. I made some good friends. Nicky was also training to be a nurse there, which was why I went for the job, but, although we saw each other almost every day at work, our relationship was never as it had been in that first flush of young love. The last time I saw her was two years later at her wedding. Six months earlier, her sister Dilly had drowned in a boating accident in Canada. Her mother had asked me to go to the funeral, but I just couldn't face it, so, when Nicky's wedding invitation plopped through the post, I knew I had to go, even though it would be difficult. I was glad that I did though; she looked so beautiful and full of life, and after so much sadness, it was wonderful to see her so happy.

On my 19th birthday I was invited to a party by a staff nurse from the X-ray department, where I'd been working for the previous three months. Liz was short, gently-spoken and very pretty. I had spoken to her often in the department, but there was never anything in it apart from work, well, that's what I had thought anyway. I did not know many other people at her party, but I stayed until the end. We had not said much to each other during the evening, but towards the end, when most people had gone, I was sitting in the garden next to the remains of the barbecue fire. She came up to me and asked if I had enjoyed the party. I said yes, it had been fun, and I thanked her for inviting me. She sat down next to me and, without saying anything else, leaned her head on my shoulder. I stayed motionless for a few moments. I did not really know how to respond. The truth was that I was frightened witless.

The abuse I had suffered had made me desperately scared of physical contact. I felt awkward and clumsy. For a while we sat there, saying nothing. Then, as if guided by a force I could not see, I took hold of her hand and held it tight. She did not recoil, she did not speak, she just leaned towards me and kissed me gently on the cheek. Over the next few weeks, I spent more and more time with her. I would see her at lunch in the staff canteen almost every day. She would either come and sit with me, or ask me to join her and whoever she was with. I grew very fond of her and found myself thinking of little else. I began to tell her more about myself, not about the abuse, but about my earlier life. She asked me about previous girlfriends. I told her about Nicky. Liz knew who she was, but didn't know her to speak to.

Towards the end of December, she asked me what I was doing over Christmas. I said I had no plans, but I wouldn't be going home. She asked me if I would like to spend it with her at her flat as she would be working on Christmas Day so she wasn't going home either. It was the beginning of what would become the first period of normality in my life since I was 14. Liz helped me through my difficulty with physical contact. She was patient and loving, and when we eventually made love for the first time, she did everything she could to help me overcome my fear, shyness and inexperience.

A month or so later, Liz asked me if I would like to move in with her. There were four other nurses in the flat and they all had boyfriends who spent a good deal of time there, especially at weekends. I jumped at the chance. It was the best thing that could have happened to me and I spent the next 18 months without a worry in the world. We went camping together in Greece in the summer. It was quite magical and, although her parents did not like the idea of us living together, they never mentioned it when ever we went to see them.

Sadly, for me anyway, Liz was offered a chance to work in a hospital in Innsbruck, something she had always wanted to do as she loved to ski. I couldn't ski to save my life, nor could I speak German, whereas Liz was almost fluent. We agreed it was too good an opportunity for her to miss, and, after all, it would only be 'for six months'. I went out to see her the following Christmas. It was a disaster. I moped about like a lost child while she did her best to make me feel wanted. Things had changed and we both knew it. A while later, she wrote to me saying she had met someone else and that she wanted to stay on for another six months. In my heart I knew it was all over. I cried for days.

Rejection is not easy for anyone, but for victims of abuse it can be especially difficult as the impact can be magnified disproportionately, often leading to self-destructive behaviour. In my case, as is not uncommon with victims of sexual abuse, I became extremely promiscuous and began to drink excessively. Over the next three years I changed jobs frequently and had one affair after another, often with women much older than I was. I felt safe with older women and less vulnerable to rejection. Looking back, I can see now that I was just desperate for affection, sex being a way to pretend that I was loved. In reality, I had become sterile in emotional terms, incapable of sharing any real feelings. I had hidden my ability to care deep in my mind to avoid being hurt.

I got a job driving a truck for an international haulage firm. It took me all over Europe and to parts of the Middle East. I met many people, some kind, some not so kind, but I managed to steer clear of people who wanted to harm me. It was a fascinating time, but driving a vehicle over long distances, alone, can be very soul destroying and I was often desperately lonely. After finding myself stuck in Calais, waiting for the ferries to run again, on two successive birthdays, I decided I just wanted to go home and stay there. But where was home?

Back in London, I met a girl called Rosemary. She had also been a nurse at St Thomas'. I new her vaguely from my time there and we began to go out together. She was kind, funny and gregarious. She introduced me to lots of her friends, and we got on well to begin with. After a couple of months, our relationship became intimate. It was more difficult than I had thought it would be. I had grown fond of her. It was not like it had been with the other women I had slept with over the previous couple of years after Liz had left. I was falling in love, and that was dangerous.

Despite the conflict within me, I continued to see her, all the time pretending that things would be all right. She knew nothing of the past, so why should she need to be told? I could start afresh, a clean slate, a new beginning. I was wrong. It wasn't long before I was sleeping with other women as well. It was only a matter of time before she found out, but I didn't care. It was as if part of me didn't want to be happy. Happiness was something beyond my understanding. I still hurt so much inside, I was incapable of holding onto anything emotional.

Rosemary had a sister, five years her senior. She ran a nursing home outside of London and Rosemary went to work for her. I stayed in London, but visited her most weekends. I got on well with her sister, and after a couple of months, she offered me a job as a gardener's assistant. The job was not well paid, but it came with free accommodation at the home. It was June, summer was in the air. I took the job and moved out of London. The home had large grounds with acres of grass and formal gardens. I spent the next two months mowing the lawns by day and drinking and dancing by night with my new-found friends. It was bliss, but a dark storm was brewing in this country idyll.

My feelings for Rosemary began to wane as I grew fonder of her sister. It could never have had a happy ending, but I continued regardless. As my relationship with Rosemary's sister developed, it became obvious to others and the whispering began. Before long, the truth was out and all hell broke loose. The end came swiftly and dramatically, and I was on the run again, unable to cope with the disaster I had created.

My parents were living in Bristol now so I called my mother, told her what had happened at the nursing home and asked if I could come and stay with them for a while until I could find a job and some digs. To my surprise she agreed, so I went home for the first time in many a year, taking with me my faithful dog, Tikka, my leaving present from Liz.

I stayed for a few months, during which time I got a job as a trainee spares compiler at British Aircraft Corporation in Filton, and moved into a small flat at the top of a large, grey Victorian house, not far from Bristol Zoo. Despite the trouble I had caused, Rosemary kept in touch and we saw each other a few times. She was a strong woman, and she had always competed fiercely with her sister. In time, she said she wanted to try again. I could not find it in my heart to hurt her a second time, so I agreed and she moved in with me. I should have been stronger, but I wasn't. Before long I asked her to marry me. I was 23, she was 24.

We were married in Clifton Cathedral. It was a wonderful day, but I knew from the moment Rosemary joined me on the steps of the main altar that this marriage was doomed. It was not me she was marrying, it was the idea of being married. The honeymoon was a disaster, and it set the scene for the remainder of our troubled marriage. Shortly afterwards, we moved south again and bought a small house in Guildford. I transferred my job to British Aircraft Corporation at Weybridge, while Rosemary went back to work at her sister's nursing home near Bramley. Eighteen months later, after endless rows, sexual problems, excessive drinking, violent outbursts, and continuous interference from her mother, we were divorced.

It was during the final few months of this miserable episode that I met Barbara. She too was married at the time, but not happily. We quickly found that we had much in common; the longing to be loved being one of the strongest desires that emerged from the hours we spent together walking in the woods on Farley Heath. By the time I knew for certain that there was nothing left between Rosemary and me, Barbara and I had become inseparable. I knew I had fallen in love with her, and, for only the second time in my life, the person I had fallen in love with told me that she loved me too! On a beautiful sunny afternoon, during a long walk in the bluebell-filled woods, not far from Barbara's home in the Surrey Hills, we decided we would run away together and build a new life of our own, free from grief and misery, and filled with children, something else we both longed for.

We secretly rented a house in Ash vale, a few miles west of Guildford, and on the chosen day, we packed some clothes and a few pots and pans and moved in together. It was summertime – it was blissful. The explosion that erupted, once it was discovered that we had fled, was loud, but we did not care. Enough was enough. We had moved on. For good or ill, we had made our choice and we would live with it, whatever the consequences. In time, of course, the fuss died down and life among those we had left behind assumed its normal irregular heart beat once more. Nine glorious months later, Barbara was pregnant. Six months after that, as soon as our divorces came through, we were married at Guildford register office. It was the day after my 26th birthday, and, despite an attack of the stomach cramps that kept me in the loo for an hour, we set off, at lunch time and I took my beautiful, heavily pregnant bride-to-be to seal our promises of love and friendship. It was by far my happiest day for many a year. Barbara looked so gorgeous, dressed in a long, white, flowing, cotton dress from Laura Ashley, and clutching a circular pose of freesias that I had constructed for her in true Blue Peter style to help hide the bump in her tummy a little! I felt deep in my soul that, this time, this relationship would last. What I could not know then was the hurt I would cause her through the years ahead as the demons from my past slowly leaked their poison out of the depths of my mind, where I had buried them away, into my living memory, tormenting , torturing, destroying. But that was in the future. For now it was a joyous, happy time.

In the years that were to follow, there would be great joy and great sorrow, but not all in equal measure. Twenty six years later, we are still married. We have three wonderful grown-up children and one grandson.

Barbara has always supported me, in spite of all the pain and heartache I have caused her. Her tenacity, common sense, steadfastness in the face of adversity, and her strong Christian faith, have been the cement that held it all together. It would be many years before I could tell her what had happened to me, but when I did, she was wonderful. She is a brave and kind woman. I owe her everything and I love her dearly.

Chapter 6

The Demons Return

Although I had been labelled as an academic disaster, something I myself had also come to believe, having had it rammed down my throat so many times, I did have talents. I was a natural communicator and I could write creatively. What I had never really appreciated was just how powerful those talents were, when harnessed. Having been treated as either an object or a failure for most of my life, my-self esteem was very low. Success was what happened to other people, not to me. But all that changed in 1975, while I was still married to Rosemary, when I met a young soldier who had broken his neck in a training accident. He was a patient at Rosemary's sister's nursing home. I spent many hours visiting him, during which time we talked about his time as a soldier. He was not much older than me, but had done so much more than I had. He had a particular interest in war planes, something I knew a good deal about. He suggested I should contact the editor of a history magazine he was reading, and offer to write for them.

I did, and to my amazement, they commissioned me to write an article about the Hawker Typhoon, a British fighter bomber that caused havoc to the German forces in the Second World War during the battle for the Falaise Gap in France. I spent three weeks researching and writing the piece, using a battered old typewriter I bought for £3 in a second-hand shop to produce the final manuscript. I posted it off and waited. I heard nothing for two months, but then, on one fine morning, a large brown envelope flopped through the flap in the front door. Inside was my article – featured on the magazine's front cover, and a cheque for £75! I could hardly believe my own eyes. I was so elated that I began writing about other military aircraft, and, the more I wrote, the more I got published. I had at last found something I really enjoyed doing, and there seemed no shortage of people wanted to pay me for doing it!

Having unlocked a skill that I had not known was there, the boy dubbed a 'failure' by his teachers began earning a living writing for other people who either couldn't write for themselves, or didn't have the time. Brochures, newsletters, company histories, speeches, leaflets, news articles, press releases, reports, plans, manuals – a million words for a million reasons, important, no doubt, to the people who commissioned them, but not really that important in the wider scheme of things.

But the words in this book are different. I have written them for a very important reason – to help other victims of sexual abuse understand that they are not alone, they are not freaks, they are not to blame for what happened to them, and their suffering was, and still is, very real. Most important of all, it is to show them that they too can make the journey from being a victim to becoming a survivor; an important part of which being the struggle for justice. It is a difficult journey, and there are those for whom the pain proves too much. It is as much in their honour that I have written this book as it is to help those who are still suffering.

For all victims of abuse, the need to survive is the driving force that shapes your life. Your brain develops coping strategies, often without you realising it. These strategies help you forget the past, but they are also harmful. I developed a complex range of strategies based on more than one personality. On the outside I was someone else, the life and soul of the party, the joker. On the inside I was a mess; my 'black' heart beat on and the nightmares were never far away. When I was with other people, I wore my mask, but when I was alone, I drank heavily, harmed myself and fought with my demons, all of which led to long periods of depression and self-loathing.

Deep within me, I had developed a desperate longing to be loved. The loss I felt for Nicky and Martin was ingrained in my soul, and the bitterness I felt towards Madley and the Salesian priests who had betrayed me continued to ferment in my heart. The combination of these emotions evolved into a subconscious hatred for injustice, which, oddly enough, manifested itself in a way that caused me even more suffering – the inability to say no. Such was my fear of causing others to suffer, I began to take upon my shoulders the problems of anyone who happened upon me in my journey through life, and, inevitably, this also made me very vulnerable to further exploitation.

I could fill many pages dwelling on this period of my life, but it would not really further the purpose of this book, suffice to say that in my travels, despite my hatred of injustice, I still managed to hurt many people. In some cases, I have been able to say sorry and make amends, but not in all, so let me say sorry now to those whose life I entered in joy, but left in sadness. You deserved much more than I could give you, and I am truly sorry that I caused you sorrow. It was not entirely my fault, as you now know, but I am still sorry.

Let me now then move to October 1996, when the dark, sinister memories I had hidden deep in my mind emerged from the background and began to haunt me again. I'd been hired to write a newsletter for a high-security psychiatric hospital. It was a new subject for me, but the task itself was similar to work I had done for many other organisations, and I soon learnt the special language necessary to make sense of the stories I was expected to research and write about. I didn't need to be a psychiatrist to do the task, but I did need to be able to spell it.

For a couple of months, the job went well. The people I worked with were doing a difficult task in a very demanding and dangerous environment. The pressures were tangible, but not overly burdensome to deal with. Bad tempers were the most common problems I had to face. Then, one day, early in February 1997, I received a telephone call and was told to come to the hospital immediately. When I got there, I was briefed about a serious problem facing the hospital. A child of eight had been brought to the hospital on a number of occasions by her father, a former patient himself, to visit another patient on the same ward. An allegation had been made by a third patient that suggested the child had been sexually abused in the hospital during those visits. The Government had become aware, as had the media. The public at large were about to find out. I was stunned; there is no other way to describe my reaction. I was asked if I would join the hospital's press office team to help them deal with the media frenzy they envisaged was about to engulf them. Why I agreed still beats me, even now looking back, but agree I did.

Over the days and weeks that followed, I worked at the hospital every day, helping draft news releases, answer press calls, and write briefing notes for the staff to keep them informed of what was happening. A police investigation began and a judicial inquiry was set up under the chairmanship of a retired judge. It was the most difficult and harrowing job I've ever had, partly because of the nature of the allegations, which reminded me very acutely of my own abuse, and partly because the atmosphere became very hostile as people began to take sides, blame each other, or simply crack up under the strain. I too began to feel the strain. But for me in particular, there was worse to come, much worse.

It started to go wrong towards the end of the summer of 1997 after a series of difficult exchanges between myself and some of the management team at the hospital. Things were said that I found degrading, threatening and hard to deal with. It all sparked off a period of increasing confusion in my mind. I became irritable, tired and short-tempered. I started drinking heavily again and found it difficult to sleep. As the weeks went by, I lost interest in my work and I found myself thinking back more and more to the events of 30 years before. Memories of the abuse kept popping into my mind. It got worse and I began thinking of little else. It was as if the experience at the hospital had triggered off a process that was unlocking the nightmares I had hidden deep in my mind in a box I had marked 'DO NOT OPEN – EVER'.

When I did fall asleep, I started to have troubling dreams, often involving replays of the abuse. Physical symptoms began to emerge such as night sweats, headaches and palpitations. I became tearful and would cry without warning. I also became very sensitive to criticism and loud noises. I felt increasingly threatened by imaginary problems. I would cross the road to avoid people, especially men. My short-term memory also deteriorated to the point where I would put a kettle on to boil and then walk away and do something else, completely forgetting the kettle. I was in trouble and I knew it. I just didn't understand what the problem was.

In November, the hospital, now under new management, rang me up one afternoon and told me that my services were no longer required. I reminded them that I had a contract which entitled me to three month's notice. They told me they were not going to give me any notice. I hadn't done anything wrong, I was just seen as connected to the old guard, and they were all being replaced. The feelings of betrayal I'd experienced at school, when I was not allowed back after I failed my exams, flooded back. I wanted someone to pay, but who, and how?

For the next 18 months, I struggled on, but I found it increasingly difficult to motivate myself and work became hard to find. I began to borrow money to service existing debts and pay the mortgage. The spiral of decline was now in full flood and my mood swings became more marked by the day. I would spend hours sitting in my study gazing at my computer screen unable to type a single word. I had also become impotent. It was as if I was dead.

Then, something happened that, although not obvious to me at the time, set in motion the changes in my mind that were to unlock my prison and set me free. My beautiful Rory, our first-born, my treasure, my little boy, the child I loved so much and had tried so hard to protect from the evils I had endured, left home to go to university. It was September 1998. The loneliness inside me grew like a cancer. I was bereft, empty and drained of all emotion. It was as if he had taken my very soul with him.

One day, I went into his room at the top of the old farmhouse where we lived and sat on the floor. I could feel his presence and it gave me comfort. I opened one of his drawers and took out a grey sweater he used to wear. I put it on and sat on his bed. All the memories of this dear little boy walked their way in procession through my mind. He was not gone, he was just away. For the next five days, I spent every minute in that room, painting it from top to bottom, making new shelves and picture frames, hoovering, dusting, tidying. I bought new rugs and lampshades, new lights for his bedside table, and when that was done, I made him a new bed. It was my way of showing him that, while I knew he had to go, this was his home, he would always be welcome here.

It was during these quiet few days, alone in that room, that I tried to make sense of what was happening to me. When it was over, I knew what I had to do. I knew who was to blame. I knew the way out. I rang my father and told him that I was thinking of writing an article about my school days, and wondered if he still had any old photos or school reports that I could look at. He said he thought he still had 'a few letters' in the loft somewhere. He would dig them out and send them to me.

Three days later, a package arrived, addressed in his handwriting. To my amazement, inside were all of my school reports, right back to primary school, hand-written first drafts of the letters he had sent to the school over the years, and all of their replies, most of which I had never seen before. They were all collated in chronological order and I began to read through them. When I reached my Christmas term report from year four, there was Madley's handwriting in the section on my performance for Physics and Chemistry. The words on the document in front of me had been written by his hand. The same hand that had abused me, time after time after time. I looked at the words and my eyes filled with tears. The floodgates opened and I wept. It was as if he was right there, standing in front of me. As my tears poured onto the page and mingled with the ink, I screamed out loud: 'You're going to pay for this, you bastard. You're fucking well going to pay.'

After a while I stopped crying. I turned on my computer, logged into a search engine and typed in the name of the school. Seconds later I was looking at pictures of my old school, the names of the current teaching staff, a guest book filled with the names and details of old boys, including boys in my cohort. I rattled off an e-mail to a few of them asking if they had any school photos of year 4A. Two hours later, a reply from a boy who had sat only a few feet away from me in class appeared in my mailbox. It had an attachment. It was another hour before I summoned the courage to open the attachment. I knew what it was. I knew what it would contain. I was frightened again. I pressed the download command. The computer responded and, there before me, a black and white photo appeared – all my old classmates, my teachers, my abuser, and me. I felt sick and turned the computer off.

Later that afternoon, I phoned a friend of mine, Stephen Wilde. He was a solicitor.

'Could I come and see you on a rather difficult personal matter?'

'What's it about?' I began to tell him roughly about the things that had happened, but after ten minutes, he said: 'Why don't you write it all down and then come and see me?'

For the next three days, I wrote and wrote and wrote. On the fourth day I went to see Stephen. It took him twenty minutes to read through the document. When he'd reached the end, he put it down and looked at me. 'I just don't know what to say. It's just so hard to imagine what it must have been like all these years living with this.'

'What should I do?' I asked.

'Sue the bastard,' said Stephen. 'And sue the bloody school as well, and the sodding local authority. Sue them all.'

Before I could say anything more, he took out a piece of paper and began scribbling furiously and barking questions at me. 'What's the school's full address? 'Who's the current headmaster?' 'Who's the current Director of Education at the Council?'

'What are you going to do?' I said.

'I'm going to write to them and ask them for the names of their insurance companies – that usually gets a prompt response!' In the meantime, you need to get a proper medical assessment – you're obviously suffering from all this and we need to know exactly what the problems are.'

'I'll make an appointment with my GP,' I said. I thanked him for listening. It had been obvious during the meeting that he had found what I had to say uncomfortable, but there was now anger in his eyes. I knew he would help me. We shook hands and he showed me out.

Chapter 7

Pandora's Box

Dr Dolan is a wonderful human being. There is really no other way to describe her. She illuminates a room when she enters. She is also a brilliant GP. I started to tell her my tale of woe. After 15 minutes she stopped me and said that there was no way we were going to get to the root of the problem that morning.

'There just isn't time and you've seen the queue out there!' I agreed and said I'd come back tomorrow.

'No', she said, 'I need to understand more about your history before I can help you so I'll arrange for you to see Helen Jones, our Community Psychiatric Nurse. She will talk to you in some detail and then tell me what's wrong!'

Two weeks later, I had my first appointment with Helen. I had never met a guardian angel before. It was a powerful experience for me; the first of many more I would have in the journey that lay ahead, not all of which would I look back on with the same feelings. Helen took me to a consulting room and sat me down. She talked a little about her role as a CPN and then asked me to tell her what the problem was.

'Take your time,' she said. 'There is no hurry.' I began to spill out my story all over again. I was doing OK until I got to the part when dear Martin's father had asked me if I would serve at Martin's requiem mass, alongside his brother Paul. When I'd first written it down in the account I prepared for Stephen, it was just words on paper. But now I was saying out loud, it seemed so real, as if I were back there on the day. I felt my bottom lip beginning to give. I began to cry, it was such a relief. I sobbed and sobbed. I just couldn't stop it. It was as if all the pain of all those years had suddenly broken through the dam and nothing could hold it back.

Helen waited patiently until I'd stopped crying and then handed me a small box of tissues. I pulled one out and dried my eyes.

'Do you want to stop?'

'No, I'm OK. There's not much more to the story anyway.' I told about the other periods of abuse, and then described all the problems I was having now. When I'd finished, she looked at for a moment, then began to speak, gently, but with command.

'Graham, I am fairly certain from what you have told me that you are suffering from Post Traumatic Stress Disorder. I think you may also have an underlying depressive illness. We can fix both of these problems, but it is going to take some time.' She picked up her phone and called Dr Dolan. They talked for a while, then Helen took me into Dr Dolan's room and said goodbye.

'Right,' said Dr Dolan. 'I'm going to put you on a course of Fluoxetine, you might know it better as Prozac. It will sort out the underlying depression. It normally takes a couple of weeks to fully kick in, but you should begin to feel a change within a few days. You will need to take it for at least six months, but don't worry, that's not a problem. My main concern right now is your blood pressure. How long has it been this high?'

I didn't know. I couldn't remember the last time I'd had it checked.

'Well, if we don't do something about it soon,' she said, 'you won't need the Prozac because you'll be dead!' I laughed and felt much calmer.

'I will also write to the Psychology Department at St. Catherine's Hospital and we'll get you on a course of trauma counselling. They're very good and they have a guy who specialises in sexual trauma. He'll help you understand exactly what has caused the past to re-emerge, and what needs to be done to put it back in its box. Helen will review you every four weeks to monitor your progress.'

Dr Dolan tapped some details into her computer and the printer churned out a prescription.

'Take one Prozac capsule and one Aprovel tablet every morning. The Aprovel will start to bring your blood pressure down to normal levels in a day or two. Any problems, just call me.' I thanked her and made my way to the nearest chemist.

A few weeks later, I received a letter from the hospital asking me if I would attend their Psychology Department for an assessment. I replied the same day, but it was another three months before they wrote to confirm a date for an appointment with a behavioural psychologist called Paul Keenan, who would assess me.

Paul was nothing like I had imagined him to be. Short and Scouse with a broad smile, a broken front tooth and constantly flicking his hair with his right hand. I quickly grew to like this man, his no-nonsense way of dealing with the issues was a source of great help to me. He was also a Roman Catholic, so he understood from his own first-hand experience the complexity of the problems involved.

Paul asked me to tell him the whole sad story. As I relived my journey to hell and back for him, he took copious notes. When I'd finished, he didn't say anything for a while, reading and re-reading his notes. Eventually, he put down the pad and looked at me for a moment as he gathered his thoughts.

'Your story is sadly not unique, Graham, except for you, of course. It is very much unique for you. No child should have to be exposed to such awful experiences, yet, it is far from uncommon. The only benefit from that, if you can call it a benefit, is that we are beginning to understand the impact of childhood sexual abuse, because we are constantly being faced with people like you, adults who were abused as children, who, now, much later in life, are victimised again by the re-emergence of the traumas suffered. We call the problems you are currently going through simply the "crisis", because that's exactly what it is. We can help you overcome this crisis, but it will take time, and before I can work out a programme to help you specifically, I need to understand in more detail how you felt in the past, and how you feel now.' Paul reached over and handed me a document.

'Don't read this now, take it home and work on it over the next few days. It's a list of questions. I want you to answer them frankly, and in as much detail as you think appropriate. Post it back to me when you've finished and I'll call you for another appointment.' He shook my hand warmly and led me out to the reception area. I made my way home, confused, but happy. I felt that I was at last beginning to make some sense of all this pain.

I didn't look at the questionnaire for two days. I just felt so washed out; the thought of having to write down my story yet again seemed like a mountain I just did not want to face. In fact, when I did read the document, and saw the logic of the questions, I found that writing down the answers was a cathartic process in itself. Each question had a score attached to it. When I'd finished and looked at my answers in relation to the score sheet, it showed that my answers gave the evidence necessary to substantiate a diagnosis of Post Traumatic Stress Disorder, with the degree of the impact on me being classed as 'Extreme'. At least I knew for sure what was wrong, and it frightened me. I posted the completed questionnaire back to Paul that afternoon.

A couple of weeks later, he wrote to me saying that he had shown the document to a colleague, Derek Farrell, who had just helped set up a newly formed counselling group at Barnardo's in Liverpool for men who had been sexually abused. He recommended that I should make contact with him, which I did, but it would be another three months before I got to see this man. By now it was becoming clear that the NHS, reflecting society in general, was not geared to dealing with adult males who had suffered childhood sexual abuse. It was a new problem that no-one seemed to want to get to grips with.

The Roman Catholic Church, of course, had other reasons for wanting the subject to remain off the agenda of public and social debate. Over the coming months though, the dam would begin to crack and the suffering of thousands upon thousands of young children, abused and betrayed by those who were responsible for their care and well-being, would start to flow. What began as a trickle would become a torrent, washing away the Roman Catholic authority, not just in the UK, but in countries such as the USA, Australia and Ireland, countries that proudly claimed to be the among the most just and civilised in the world. The Roman Church would be rocked to its very foundations, and, little, insignificant me would be right in the middle of it all.

On 12 June 2000, I finally met Derek. He was tall, good-looking and extremely confident, and he put me instantly at ease. I found going through my story with him less difficult than on previous occasions, but perhaps I was just getting used to telling it. Derek listened carefully, but after a while he seemed to become distracted. It was obvious that he had something else on his mind. When I'd finished, he said this first session was just so we could get to know each other and that the real work would begin next time. He proposed ten sessions, one a week for about an hour. I thanked him and he showed me out.

The next meeting, on 19 June, was the last time I ever saw him. During the session, I did most of the talking, which ranged from my problems with alcohol to the painful and frightening subject of whether or not I would become an abuser myself because I had been abused. Derek's mobile phone went off several times during the conversation and he would make excuses and leave the room to answer the phone. Each time he came back in, he looked perplexed and distant. I felt very vulnerable and began to wish I wasn't there. Before the hour was up, while I was still talking, Derek suddenly said he had to cut it short because he had another appointment, but he would see me again in a week and we could pick up from there. I was confused and annoyed, but relieved it was over.

On 23 June, I received a short letter from his secretary saying the appointment was cancelled as Derek was unavailable until further notice. 'We will be in touch again at the earliest opportunity with an alternative appointment.' I was shattered. Only a few days ago, I had been talking to this man about some of the blackest and most frightening thoughts that lurked in the darkest regions of my mind. Why? Because he had said he could help. Now he was gone. No goodbye, no explanation, just gone.

A month later, I received a letter from Paul Keenan. It said simply that Derek Farrell was no longer with the department and I was to contact Barnardo's in Liverpool myself to make arrangements to attend the Men's Group. He ended the letter with the words 'Good luck'. A week later, having tried unsuccessfully to make contact with the facilitator of the group, I wrote to Paul to try and explain how I now felt about the whole situation. I said that the unexplained circumstances surrounding Derek's abrupt departure had left me feeling confused and disturbed. I said that the feelings of being let down again were strong at the moment, but that I was trying to be as objective as I could about it.

A few days later, I saw Helen Jones again. When I told her what had happened, she was so concerned that she telephoned Derek Farrell's secretary and asked her to find me another psychotherapist to continue the therapy Derek had begun.

On 14 August, I received a reply, not from Paul, but from his boss, Austin Sinnott, the Clinical Director. He apologised sincerely on behalf of the Directorate for the 'inevitable emotional consequences for yourself,' and said he would arrange for me to be seen as a priority for one-to-one psychological therapy. He did, and finally, on 18 September, I began an intensive course of therapy with Paul Keenan, which really helped me make sense of the past and overcome some, but not all, of the fears it had left me with.

A central part of the therapy involved a treatment called EMDR (Eye Movement Desensitisation and Reprocessing). Developed by an American psychologist, Dr Franchine Shapiro, EMDR was proving to be of considerable help in cases for victims with anxiety based disorders, and disorders that have their basis in emotional trauma in earlier years.

Paul had just begun to introduce the treatment and he was as keen as I was to try it on me based on positive reports of its success. Before we began, he warned me that I might find EMDR therapy difficult as it involved exploring deep into my memory and drawing out in very minute detail what had happened. I even had to sign a disclaimer saying that if it made things worse, I wouldn't sue them! Despite this, I trusted Paul and we got on with it.

The purpose of EMDR is to enable painful memories to be re-filed in your memory in such a way that they become less likely to pop into your mind when you don't want them to. The treatment requires you to close your eyes and focus on three main aspects of the trauma: firstly, a visual image, which is usually an image you associate with the most disturbing part of the trauma; secondly, the negative thought you have about yourself in relation to the trauma; and, thirdly, the location of the disturbance in your body. You then open your eyes and follow the therapist's finger as it tracks back and forward across your visual field in rapid, saccadic eye movements.

After each set of movements, you report what you are experiencing. As the process continues, you notice a decrease in the emotional impact of the trauma memory. This decrease can be gradual, or, in some cases, dramatic.

You may also notice, as I did, that your perception of your own part in the trauma changes. Abreaction can also occur, which is where disturbing memories that have been forgotten or repressed suddenly come to the surface, often accompanied by the release of more painful memories.

The part of the trauma I focused on was the time in the derelict cottage in Wales where Madley raped me. The image of the fire in the range was so clear, I could even feel the heat. The negative thought I focused on was the feelings I had during that terrible episode of being weak and feeble and unable to help myself. The location of the disturbance in my body was my stomach, the place I suffered those terrible cramps for years afterwards.

For the next few months, Paul counselled me once a week for an hour. Although painful and challenging, the process did work. I recommend it to other victims as I can now think about what happened to me in a much more rational way without it triggering the kind of symptoms from which I had previously suffered.

Paul had also recommended that I should still go along to the men's group at Barnardo's in Liverpool as he felt it would help me as I would learn about coping with the impact of abuse directly from others who had gone through similar ordeals. The group had been established by the charity following the North Wales Care Home abuse cases which had highlighted the need for such support. I joined and attended the Group which also met once a week.

'Sad school', as my children named it, was also very helpful to me. The discussions in the group were never easy, but because we all shared the same awful experience, there was a natural trust between us from the start, which enabled each member of the group to say things that we found so difficult to say to anyone else, even to our individual therapists, more easily. The facilitator who ran our group, Peter Harmsworth, is a remarkable man. His mild manner and quietly spoken tones acted as the centre pin in our troubled world that kept us all safe. He ensured that, no matter how emotional, frustrated and angry we got, our dignity was never at risk. He is a brave and highly skilled family therapist, and I owe him a great deal, as do we all in the group.

One thing I learnt, very soon after joining the group, that really surprised me, was the degree of compassion victims of abuse are able to show each other. I had wrongly thought such groups would be driven by self pity, but that was not the case. Despite their ordeals, and these men all had terrible tales to tell of their appalling treatment, some of which was far worse than the abuse I had suffered, their courage and kindness was humbling, and they have been a great source of healing. I only hope that through my contribution I was able to help them in some small way as well.

Chapter 8

Breaking the Silence

In the months of waiting for the counselling with Paul Keenan, I had also begun another vital phase in my struggle to recover – the battle for justice. This was to prove far more testing than anything I had experienced during therapy, and, had I known that at the outset, I would not have had the courage or the strength to carry on. Sometimes, the saying 'ignorance is bliss', can work in your favour rather than against you.

The conclusion I had come to at the end of my week in Rory's room was that I would have to confront the school once more with what had happened to me, but this time I would stand in front of them as a man, not as a child. This time I would make them listen to me and apologise for failing me so badly. I was convinced that I would never fully recover from my ordeal until I had resolved the unfair way I had been dealt with by the school and others. The sense of betrayal had so stained my character that I had come to view almost everyone and everything in life with suspicion and doubt. If I was going to move on, I would have to find a way of resolving that.

I still carried in my heart anger and hatred for Madley, the school and everyone who had ever let me down. That anger had long since ceased to be the fiery rage that we all feel when things go wrong. It was a dark anger that had become tempered by time, like steel. It was cold, intense and deadly. I could use it now to save me, or I could let it go on etching into my soul until the day came when it would inevitably destroy me. As I wrestled with this terrifying conundrum, I weighed up all the possible outcomes. I drew up a list of all the bad outcomes and all the good outcomes. The bad included the way people might think of me when they found out. The good included the possibility that if I told my story, others might also be able to tell theirs.

By the time I had written down all of the possible scenarios I could think of, good and bad, the answer began to emerge; I would break the silence I had kept for all these years and take the consequences like a man. It was time to stop being frightened. It was now or never. I would find a way to challenge Madley, if he was still alive, and the school, and force them to acknowledge the damage they had done to me. But I would also challenge them further. I would ask them to prove to me that what happened to me could not happen to other boys now. After all, wasn't the Roman Catholic Church trying to show the world that it had changed its ways and would not tolerate anyone who abused children?

A few days after I had gone to see Dr Dolan that first time, Stephen, the solicitor, had phoned me to say that his letter to my old school had certainly stirred up a hornet's nest, but not quite in the way he had expected. Their reply, via their solicitors, was to inform him that they had 'no record of any incident' involving me, and, further, they had no record of any teacher with the name I had supplied ever working at the school. I searched through my old school reports and the letters my father had sent me, which revealed the correct spelling of Madley's name. I had spelt his surname with an additional 'e'- Madeley – hardly enough to warrant their 'no record of any teacher' response – but enough to show us that we had a fight on our hands.

I was determined to make the school take me seriously this time. Stephen advised me to make a formal complaint to the police. He told me there is no time limit in criminal law on sexual offences, and, as I was under 16 when Madley assaulted me at the cottage, he could face a long prison sentence if he were convicted – even life in prison.

'That will get them thinking,' he said.

I put the phone down and began writing a letter to the police. I felt a growing sense of empowerment as I typed. It was my turn to exercise power now, and there was nothing they could do to stop me.

By now, I was able to write my story without feeling so completely overwhelmed, although it was still difficult to read the words as they appeared on the screen in front of me. I explained what had happened at school and how it had affected me. I said that I wanted to stop being a victim, and to achieve this I intended to seek redress through the civil and criminal justice system for the suffering I had endured over all these years. I attached a copy of the document I had prepared for Stephen, and said I would be happy to give them any further information they might want. I addressed the letter to the Chief Superintendent at the police station nearest to my old school, and posted it. It was done. I had lit the fuse. No more mealy mouthed letters from the school's solicitors. The gloves were well and truly off now, and I felt a sense of calm growing inside me. I was no longer fighting my battle on my own.

Three days later, I received a short letter from Sarah Harris, an officer with Surrey's Child Protection Unit at Addlestone Police Station, asking me simply to phone her. I called her as soon as I had finished reading it. Sarah introduced herself and explained that they needed to be sure it was really me they were talking to before they could discuss my allegations in any detail, which is why she had asked me to phone her. She said she had been given the task of investigating my allegations and suggested we meet at their special interview house which, although designed for interviewing children, was very private and had all the necessary recording facilities. We agreed a date and time and she said she and a colleague would collect me from the railway station at Weybridge when I arrived. Once again, it seemed, the station at Weybridge, where Martin and I always said goodbye to each other as we went our separate ways home, and greeted each other in the mornings, was to play one more vital role in the story.

The journey down was a roller-coaster of emotions. I was unsure how I would react in the interview, given the last experience I'd had with the police, but I felt happy that at last something positive was happening. I took with me my old school reports, the letters and the school photograph. At this stage I still did not know if Madley was alive or dead.

Sarah Harris was about 30, tall and quietly spoken with a soft West Country accent. Her colleague, Lorraine Smith, was a little older, not quite as tall and spoke with a harsher, northern accent. They were very unlike the two male detectives who'd interrogated me all those years ago at Woking police station. The special house, a converted police house in a quiet residential street in suburbia, was filled with toys, children's books and videos. It was perfect and I felt instantly at ease. I had met two more guardian angels.

For the next four hours, Sarah delved deep into my past, dragging out every last scrap of information about me, my family and Madley. She was a highly trained and skilful investigator. I was amazed at some of the information she was able to unlock. It was the level of detail in particular that made such an impact on me. Questions like: 'What did you use to clean up after he had abused you?' Until she'd asked me that I hadn't even thought about it.

'His hanky,' I said. 'A white hanky – I can see it now.'

Her colleague said very little during the entire interview; her unenviable task was to write down everything I said. We had to stop several times due to cramp in her fingers. In the end, when Sarah was satisfied that she had retrieved every last piece of information from my memory, she asked me if there was anything I wanted to ask her.

'There is something that still bothers me,' I said. 'From all that I've told you, do you feel in any way that I was to blame for what happened? Could I have stopped it from happening sooner?' Sarah looked at me for a moment and said: 'Graham, you were a child. He was an adult and your teacher. What else could you have done in reality? Nothing. He is entirely guilty for what he did to you. It was not within your power to stop him. You were not to blame in any way whatsoever, and that's all there is to say about it.'

I began to cry, more out of relief that it was all out in the open, but partly because of the image burning in my mind, the image of me staring back at myself from the school photo. A young boy. A child. She was right. I'd done nothing to be ashamed of, yet I still felt ashamed. I gave her the photo and they took me back to the train station.

'I'll call you in a few days when we've typed up your statement. You'll have to come back to sign it if that's OK. In the meantime, we'll be making our "enquiries" as they say!' I thanked them both for the way they had conducted the interview and climbed aboard the waiting train. It had been a difficult but positive day.

It would be some time before I learnt that Sarah's "enquiries" had shaken the school to its foundations, and in doing so, she had uncovered disturbing circumstantial evidence that, on the face of it, looked very much as if the school had gone out of its way to cover up what they knew to be true, to avoid a major scandal.

With a police investigation underway, the school's solicitors suddenly became much more amenable, assuring Stephen, who was now acting officially for me, that they were not in any way trying to be obstructive when they had failed to recognise the correct name of the teacher. Now that the police were involved, however, the civil action would have to wait. No matter; we now had their full attention. Now was the time to tackle those further up the chain of responsibility. I wrote to the Director of Education, Dr Paul Gray, at Surrey County Council to ask him to set up a formal inquiry into all of the issues involved in my case.

I told him the whole story and added that I had given a statement to the police. I wanted to embarrass the council into explaining why my school had been able to get away with keeping my 'confession' hidden. I put it to him that here were fundamental questions that needed answering, such as did the school properly investigate my allegations at the time in accordance with the regulations and procedures covering such incidents? What action did the school take following their investigation? Why was I not offered counselling and support? Why were my parents not told?

Why were the police not told? Why was I told not to say anything further about it? Why was the teacher who abused me not suspended? What action was taken to ensure that this teacher did not further abuse me or any other pupil and, finally, what lessons can be learnt to ensure that what happened to me cannot happen again to others?

The council's education policy was spelt out very clearly on their web site. They proudly boasted that their 'aim for school education was to ensure that each pupil reached his or her full potential, and to secure the highest possible standards of attainment for all, through a broad and balanced school education which prepares pupils for the responsibilities and opportunities of adult life'.

I suggested to Dr Gray that it was reasonable to assume that this policy, albeit not published on a web site, was also in place in 1966, but what had happened to me severely damaged my chance to reach my full potential, denied me any opportunity of securing the highest possible standards of attainment and failed absolutely to prepare me for the responsibilities and opportunities of adult life.

'The truth is,' I told him, 'I was denied the opportunity to reach my potential, or get anywhere near reaching it, by the very people who were entrusted in law to provide me with the pastoral care, appropriate learning environment and adequate support necessary for me to thrive.' I finished by saying that I had set myself six objectives as part of my recovery process, and that I would not rest until I had achieved them all. I wanted the school to accept that I was abused, to accept that they failed to protect and support me and to accept that they had denied me the opportunity to reach my full potential. I also wanted a sincere apology, some form of compensation and an assurance with evidence that what happened to me could not happen again to others. I knew that my letter would cause them difficulties, but I also knew how devious and treacherous bureaucrats could be, so, to make sure my letter did not get 'lost in the system', I sent a copy to David Blunkett, the Secretary of State for Education.

A week went by and I had not had any response, so I wrote again to the council, and this time I also wrote to my MP, Andrew Miller, enclosing a copy of a letter I had sent to Dr Gray, and asking if he would also write to the council on my behalf and ask them what they intended to do about the issues I had raised.

On 27 January, Dr Gray replied, saying that he was very disturbed to read my letter, and that he had 'immediately referred the matter to my colleagues in Social Services whose responsibility it is to conduct investigations of this nature'. Now that I had his attention, it was time to put a spoke in the wheel. I wrote back on 31 January saying that, in preparing my case, I had discovered extensive correspondence between my father, the school, and the Chief Education Officer at the time, covering the period of the abuse and beyond it. I told him that it was very clear from this correspondence that it was obvious at the time that something was seriously wrong with my progress, yet neither the school nor the then Director of Education had given any indication to my father that I had in fact informed the school that I was being abused.

Had he been told, of course, the reason for my lack of progress would have been obvious to all, as indeed would the likely outcomes and conse-quences that would then have followed. I put it to him that, in my view, the difficulty that the discovery of this correspondence posed is that it raises the question of what exactly the Education Department did know at the time about my situation and what action it took? 'Your department clearly should not be involved in investigating itself, and I am therefore asking you to assure me that the Child Protection and Independent Review Unit does in fact have the authority to investigate independently your department's involvement in my case as well as the authority to inves-tigate the school's involvement. I am not suggesting that the Education Department did in fact know about the abuse at the time, but I'm sure you will appreciate my concerns.'

Having had no reply by 7 February, I telephoned the contact I had been referred to by Dr Gray at their Child Protection Unit, Simon Slater. He seemed uncomfortable and not really sure what to say to me.

'Basically,' he said, 'I've been given your case because it's got "child protection" written all over it, which is absolutely appropriate. We now have some procedural guidance which our area child protection committee has agreed on about how we should respond to what we describe under the general heading of complex or wide-scale abuse investigations. It's a strange heading, but never mind about that. It includes historical abuse allegations in schools, so what we are dealing with from you clearly falls within that.'

He spluttered on, thinking on his feet and clearly not prepared. 'Our role in social services, however, is more limited than you might have thought. There is an issue about what our appropriate role is. You are obviously asking for clarification on that in your last letter because you have specifically said "can the DE confirm that I have the authority to investigate the LEA?" Frankly, to be honest with you, I'm not sure that I have got that authority. What the DE has done is to send that letter of yours to my boss and to me saying could we advise him on a response. So that is what's going on at this moment. Perhaps I shouldn't pre-empt this, but it's my view that it is not within my authority to do that.'

I asked him to explain what the terms of reference for the inquiry were.

He said that they would liaise with the police about any information they already had and what investigations they could make. Their aim was to have a co-ordinated response with the police. He added that given the fact that I was an adult, and they were not aware at that stage of any current child protection issues in connection with my former teacher, that it would be mainly a police-led investigation. He concluded by saying that he did not yet know the name of the teacher, so I told him the name and how to spell it, and thanked him for his time.

The next day, my MP's secretary called me to ask if I had had a reply from the Director of Education. I said that I had, and I explained where things stood. She asked if I wanted a reply from the Secretary of State. I said that as long as he was aware of my case, that was OK. She said that he was aware, wished me luck and said goodbye.

Later that day, I wrote to Simon Slater, following up our earlier conversation. I enclosed a copy of my original testimony and copies of the letters and my school reports. It was obvious from the DE's response to my first letter to him that this was the first he had known about my case, yet the school had been contacted about it by my solicitor in September 1999. This would indicate that the LEA had not been informed by the school that an investigation was underway. I said this worried me as it was a repeat of what had happened in 1968 when I first informed them. I told him that I was deeply sceptical about the way inquiries are conducted, and that I was adamant that this time those actually responsible for what happened to me would be identified, challenged and dealt with appropriately.

A week later, he sent me a copy of their procedures for investigating child abuse cases. The document was very wordy and certainly gave the appearance that child abuse was being taken seriously by local authorities. It stated that their general principles were to ensure that any necessary action is taken to secure the immediate safety of children, that the needs of the children concerned were paramount, and should inform the manner and timing of the investigation, and, subject to the requirements of full investigation and any necessary action, disruption to the establishment concerned would be kept to a minimum. It went on and on about how the relevant agencies would co-operate in assessing what was required, and that they would all work together, pooling resources where appropriate, to meet the diverse needs of individual children and groups of children . . . etc . . . etc . . . etc.

Despite the long-winded jargon most of the document contained, it ended encouragingly with this unambiguous statement: 'It is of the greatest importance that those in authority are clear that, although there may be insufficient evidence to support a police prosecution, this does not mean that action does not need to be taken to protect the child, or that disciplinary procedures should not be invoked and pursued.' Maybe the bureaucrats really had learnt the lessons of the past.

On 14 February, I received a letter from Lorraine Morris, an official with the Pupil Support and Independent Schools Division at the Department for Education and Employment. It appeared that the letter I had sent to the Secretary of State really had been read by the man himself. The letter said how very sorry they were to read about my experiences at school, and that they wanted to assure me the Government was concerned that children should be protected from abuse. Enclosed with the letter was a copy of the department's child protection guidance circular entitled 'Protecting Children from Abuse: The Role of the Education Service'. It set out the action to be taken by teachers with designated responsibility for child abuse issues, where there are suspicions that a child may be at risk from abuse. It included advice on what action should be taken if teachers or other members of staff were themselves accused of abuse. Also enclosed were two other circulars entitled 'Working Together for the Protection of Children from Abuse: Procedures within the Education Service', and 'Working Together to Safeguard Children,' a guide to inter-agency working to safeguard and promote the welfare of children.

Then, as if by way of excusing what had happened, the letter said 'Unfortunately, these policies were not in existence when you were at school.' You must be joking, I thought. What possible difference would they have made? They are certainly not making any difference today. Don't they read the press? Hardly a week goes by without the courts dealing with paedophiles in schools.

Like Pontius Pilate washing his hands as he handed Christ to be crucified, the letter concluded by saying, 'I have been assured by the Local Education Authority that all schools in the Authority, and the Authority itself, now have child protection policies which reflect the advice contained in our Circular 10/95, and the procedures set out by the local Area Child Protection Committee. I understand from them, that the child protection procedures are currently being revised and that he would be more than happy to let you see a copy in draft.' Oh, well, that's alright then. We can sleep safe in our beds in the sure knowledge that all the little children are safe. What they did not know was that at the same time that they were writing to me, at the primary school where my wife was teaching, a young male student teacher was abusing some of the children in her class. He was later arrested, prosecuted and convicted after one of the boys told his mother.

The school's head had been aware of concerns about the student expressed by my wife and other teachers who had observed his unusual fondness for the children, but she had dismissed their concerns and done nothing. So much for their policies. In my mind I had a vision of hundreds of bureaucrats, their heads in the sand, surrounded by piles of unread copies of their child protection policies, while in the background the voices of little children went unheard.

Telling them that they were living in cloud-cuckoo-land would not have helped my campaign, so, a few days later, I replied saying that I was greatly encouraged by the response I had had from the LEA and now from them. I wanted them to know that there was much still to be done, and while I was grateful for their assurances, I wanted them to know how difficult it was to resurrect the awful memories associated with this dreadful period of my life, but it had to be done if I was ever going to recover and begin to help other victims of abuse. I confirmed that I was fully prepared to go through with what I had begun, regardless of how unpleasant it might get.

On 22 February, the LEA's Service Co-ordinator, Geraldine Allen, wrote to tell me that she was now responsible for co-ordinating the investigation into my allegation of abuse, and to ensure that any out-standing child protection issues were identified and properly dealt with. She explained the process, saying that it would begin with a strategy meeting, attended by Social Services, the police, a representative from the County Council Education Department and a representative from the school. They would then detail my allegations and any action taken to date, and would plan the action required to investigate fully. They would also examine as far as possible whether my allegations gave rise to any current child protection concerns, and if so how these would be addressed. She said she would contact me again following the meeting to explain the planned course of action. It was a wonderful feeling. I had stuck a large stick in their ant hill and all the ants were running around like crazy trying to fix it up! Things had come a long, long way since Madley had said 'They don't believe you.'

The following day Sarah Harris e-mailed to say that she had completed my statement and she would like me to come down and go through it with her.

Two days later, Dr Gray wrote saying that the Child Protection and Independent Review Unit of the Social Services Department was convening a meeting to plan an investigation into the allegations I had made. He said that the LEA would be represented at that meeting and they would have to agree how to investigate the issues I had raised that would not be covered by the joint enquiry led by Social Services and the Police. Only after that discussion had occurred on 3 March could they make a decision about how to manage any enquiries which fell outside the main investigation.

He finished by saying that both the Social Services Department and the police had the authority to investigate an enquiry into all aspects of the allegations, including the previous involvement of his department with my school. 'The Education Department will co-operate fully in this matter. There are complicating factors which the LEA will have to consider. The first relates to the legal status of the School, and the second to the length of time since the alleged events took place. Any records held by the LEA will be made available to Social Services and the Police.'

On 8 March, I drove down to Addlestone Police Station and went through the nine-page typed statement with Sarah Harris. I made some minor amendments to the spelling of names, but no other changes. Reading the statement for the first time since I had made it back in November shocked me, as it was so real. There in front of me in cold print was the full account of what had happened, in all its awful detail. I found it very disturbing and we spent some time talking about the whole subject and what was still to come. Sarah was very understanding and made me feel very much at ease. She updated me on the outcome of the strategy meeting that took place on 3 March, then paused for a moment before saying that Madley was still alive. In fact, he had only recently retired from Salesian College Battersea, where he had been teaching ever since he left Salesian College Chertsey in 1968. She said she had also found my old headmaster, Fr O'Shea.

'He's also alive and living at the Salesian College in Farnborough. He's said to be a bit doddery, but Lorraine Smith and I intend to visit him soon. We will also be paying a visit to the schools at Chertsey and Battersea.'

The priest who came to interrogate me after my confession had also been identified, a Fr George Williams, a name I did not recognise at the time. There was now no going back, no recoiling from the demons I had unlocked; the bus to freedom from my nightmare was really moving now.

On 7 April, Sarah phoned to say she had been to see the head teacher at Salesian College in Battersea, Mr McCann, and got Madley's employment history and personal details.

'I have also been to see your old headmaster at Farnborough. He was very helpful, . . . well, I say helpful, but he couldn't remember anything! He made out that he was giving us all the help he could, but then said that he couldn't remember anything about what I wanted to speak to him about. Basically he has provided what we call a negative statement, i.e. saying I've been asked about this but I can't remember anything at all! So that's that.'

Sarah's next words made the hair on the back of my neck stand up.

'There are some things of concern that have come up from Battersea that we may need to look into. It would appear Madley had some sort of liaisons with pupils while he was there, but there were never any allegations made, or any concern that he was being inappropriate. That is something we will follow up aside from your allegations. So the next thing is that I will write to Mr Madley and invite him in for interview. I would imagine he has heard through the grapevine what is going on already, in fact, I am quite surprised that he has not been in touch already. I don't know about you, but I would want to know what is being said. It appears that they moved him to Battersea when you left. He's been there ever since, but interestingly there is nothing in his personnel file about anything to do with you. But then you don't know if it was swept under the carpet in those days or what, do you? I mean nowadays, God, it should be logged so carefully and there is nothing in that file, not even an explanation as to why he moved from one school to the other. You have to wonder about that as he wasn't at your school for very long, a bit more than a year maybe. The rest of his career was spent at the other school. The fact that he moved there shortly after you left is very interesting! I'll let you know how I get on with our Mr Madley.' I thanked her for everything she had done and put the phone down. I felt sick. My hands started to shake as I wrote down a note of what she had said for my record.

On 2 May, Sarah phoned to tell me that she had arrested Madley! I was almost dumbfounded when she told me.

'Yes, a bit of a shock out of the blue for you!' she said. 'I wrote him a little letter and he came on down with his solicitor to the police station, where I arrested him. We didn't get very far though because, although he was deemed fit to be interviewed by our people, his solicitor put up a bit of a fight saying he wasn't fit to be interviewed because he wasn't feeling too well. He certainly didn't look well after I started to interview him!'

Sarah said she had bailed him to re-attend in a fortnight, when she would 'have another go' at interviewing him.

'At the end of the day,' she said, 'he needs to be given a chance to answer the allegations.'

I asked her if he looked anything like he did in the school photo?

'No,' she replied, 'he is very grey and obviously a lot older. He's a wizened old man really. I'm away next week so I'll have another go the following Wednesday – two weeks tomorrow – I'll try to interview him again then. I'll call you afterwards.'

I put the phone down, punched the air with my fists and shouted out loud: 'Yes – how did you like that then, Madley, you bastard?'

Chapter 9

Justice Denied

Sarah phoned again on 18 May. It was not the news I'd prayed for, but it was what I'd half expected.

'Hello, Graham. Well, Mr Madley came along yesterday with his solicitor and we eventually interviewed him. Do you know what I am going to say next?'

'You are either going to say he denied it, or he coughed.'

'Which one do you reckon?'

'I'd like to reckon that he coughed, but I think he probably denied it.'

'Yes, that's right, but, spookily enough, a lot of the details you gave in your statement he agreed with, i.e. the trip to Wales, the home tutoring, that sort of thing, but none of the offences. He agreed with everything, but not the offences.'

'At least part of his memory still works.'

'Well, when it suits him it does. So, basically we've got your word against his, which we thought would be the case anyway. So what I've done is bailed him for six weeks and I'll be submitting an advice file to the CPS, which is the way you thought it would go.'

'Yes, that's wonderful, thank you.'

'That's all right. It could take longer than six weeks to be honest, but as soon as I know what's happening I'll let you know. I've had your criminal injuries consent forms through, so I'll send them off and get copies of your medical notes.'

'Thank you for all your help so far.'

'That's all right – no problem. It's moving forward isn't it?'

'Yes.'

'What about if they say no, it isn't going to go to court?'

'I'm prepared for that. I would proceed with the private prosecution.'

'Sure.'

'It's not going to go away, that's the thing.'

' That's right. The bloke's a wreck though, I have to say. It should make you feel a bit better to know that this thing has stressed him out no end and he's lost a lot of weight since he came in last time. He is worried!'

On 8 May, the LEA's Service Co-ordinator, Geraldine Allen, wrote informing me that they had not been able to hold the meeting they had planned for 5 May due to the police being unable to attend. They had rescheduled the meeting for 25 May and would be in contact with me again after then. I heard no more until June 27 when they wrote to say that there had been no further allegations made against Madley to date, and, consequently, they were waiting for the decision of the Crown Prosecution Service as to whether they would proceed with my case into court. They would then decide what further work should be undertaken in order to respond to my allegations.

A week later, on 3 July, Sarah rang with the news we had all been waiting for. It was the worst news in the world. She said she had received a reply from the CPS following the file she had submitted to them. It said they had carefully considered the allegations I had made but, as the police had not been able to corroborate my allegations, plus the fact Fr Madden, the priest I had first confessed to, had died, and that my old headmaster, Fr O'Shea, did not recall any such allegations being made to him, they were left simply with my evidence, which Madley had denied. Consequently, they said, they regretted that, under the circumstances, they could not see that there was a realistic prospect of conviction in this case and, accordingly, could not advise any proceedings being instituted against Madley.

So, after everything I had been through, I was to be denied even the opportunity to challenge in court the man who had destroyed me. I felt completely numb. He had got away with it again. I asked Sarah if that was the end of the road from a police point of view. She said that the file would remain with them and that my statement still stood. If something did happen further down the line, such as another witness coming forward, they would resurrect the case. However, the file would only be held there, it would not appear on the national police computer because Madley had not been convicted, so if another witness came forward in another part of the country, my allegations would not flash up when they searched the system.

I could tell from Sarah's voice that she was as distressed as I was. She had put so much effort into the investigation and it had all come to nothing. I thanked her again for everything she had done and told her that I couldn't really have got this far without her help. She wished me good luck for the future and we said goodbye. I was back to square one, alone, confused and angry. I could see him smirking. Oh, how I hated him.

On 11 July, the Head of Education Children's Services wrote to me to say that they had carried out a detailed investigation of all their historic records to see if there was anything from my school relating to me. They had found nothing and were, regrettably, unable to progress the matter further. On 31 July, I received another letter from Social Services saying that no further work could be undertaken to investigate my allegations now that the police investigation had stopped. I felt so low. The elation I had experienced when Sarah told me she had arrested Madley had evaporated as, one by one, the avenues I had explored in my search for justice had turned into dead ends. I closed my study door and went for a long walk with my faithful dog Emma. She wouldn't let me down, nor I her.

A week went by and, gradually, a new sense of purpose began to fill my mind. I was calmer now and not so despairing. The anger inside had once again gone cold, but it had not gone away. If anything, its flame was burning brighter. I decided there was still one more thing I could do to keep my fight going. I would challenge the CPS decision. So, on 7 August, I wrote to the CPS branch that dealt with my case and asked them to explain in detail why they had denied me the chance to bring my case before a judge and jury, after all, there must be dozens of cases tried by the courts every day that do not end with a conviction. Why were those cases able to go before the courts, but not mine?

On 14 August, I received a reply from the Chief Crown Prosecutor herself. At least they were taking my complaint seriously I thought when I opened the letter and saw her name on the bottom. I read it carefully, and then read it again. The detailed explanation I had asked for was exactly what I got, but it did not help me. Madley had escaped because the law, as it is written, says the defendant is more important than the victim. At least, that's the way it seemed.

The basis of their decision was that, in view of the passage of time, they would be unable to satisfy a jury to the required standard that the offences had been committed in the way that I had described, and, further, that in any event the judge would in all likelihood refuse to allow the matter to proceed on the basis that Madley could not have a fair trial. It was an abuse of the criminal process to prosecute offenders where they have been denied that basic right of a fair trial. This means that they have to be in a position to defend themselves against the allegation.

'You will appreciate,' she said, 'that over 30 years have passed, and that this is the first time Mr Madley has been faced with these allegations. Clearly, he is not in a position to put forward an effective defence. I appreciate that you, as a victim, also have rights, but the Crown Prosecution Service acts in the public interest in prosecuting rather than the interests of one individual. It would be wholly wrong to put this matter before the court in the full knowledge that, even if the Judge allowed the matter to proceed, we could not satisfy any jury to the very high standard required before they could find Mr Madley guilty.'

So then, as far as the criminal law was concerned, unless other victims came forward, that was the end of the matter. Madley had escaped justice and was free to continue, to abuse, violate and blight the lives of more young boys. God only knows how many others he had already done that to. The anger and frustration inside me grew again. I could not and would not let it end here.

Chapter 10

The Truth Will Set Me Free.

I still felt desperately lonely. I had nothing really to show for all I had been through, save the satisfaction of knowing that Madley had at least suffered the humiliation of being arrested and questioned after all these years. I was adamant that he was not going to beat me. I would find other victims, but to do that I would first have to tell the rest of the world what had happened to me.

Summer was beginning to fade. It was almost a year since I had written my original account of what had happened. On a bright, September morning, I went into my study and collected together all of the documents and correspondence I had received from everyone involved so far, including the old letters from school that my father had given me. I put them all into chronological order and began to scan them into my computer. I added all of the letters I had written, my medical notes and the original document I had written for Stephen. I then wrote an introduction to it all, and placed the entire archive on a web site I had registered under the domain name 'Victims No Longer'. I was now ready. If Madley had thought it was over, he was very wrong. It had only just begun. The little boy he had abused and betrayed all those years ago was now a man. I was no longer frightened of what he could do, or what anyone else could do for that matter. I was going to tell my story to the world, and they were just going to have to deal with the consequences.

On 6 September, I wrote once more to the Director of Education, the head of the CPS, the police and the Secretary of State for Education, to inform them of my plans. I told them that I had asked my solicitor to file a claim in the High Court against Madley and the school, and that I had written a full account of what happened and placed it on a web site, which, subject to approval from my solicitor, would be linked to the major search engines and thus be available for the world to view at will.

I told them that the purpose of the site was threefold: to help other victims of abuse find the courage to tell of their ordeals and begin the painful and difficult process of recovery; to help them understand the difficulties they could expect to face when they do inform the authorities; and to find the other victims that Madley had abused so that a successful criminal case could be brought against him, bringing an end to his reign of terror and allowing all the lost souls he had destroyed to live once more as men. I signed the letters Graham Wilmer – Victim No Longer.

I discussed the plan with Stephen, who advised that, for the time being, I should not refer to Madley by his real name on the web site. I could live with that, so I deleted all the references to him, replacing them with the letter X. Having done that, I sent an e-mail to the various search engines with the details of the site. Victims No Longer would become visible for all the world to see in a matter of hours. I had told them all that I would do it, and now I had.

But there remained one more thing to do: to tell my children what I had done and why. Up to this point, none of them knew anything about what had happened, they only knew that I had been ill. Rory was 20, Eve 17 and a half, and Zachary just 16. Not surprisingly, each took my bombshell revelation in different ways. But, once the initial shock had worn off, they were glad I had told them, and they swore that if I didn't 'nail the bastard', they would do it for me!

It was not an easy decision to tell them, but the thought of them hearing about it from someone other than me was just not in the running. As a parent, I felt I had no real choice but to tell them, and their reactions told me that I had done the right thing. It was time to release the hounds.

Within hours of the web site going live, I received an e-mail from another pupil at the school that stunned me. He said that he too had been abused, but not by Madley. He also talked of a cover-up, saying he had witnessed a regime of abuse perpetrated by a small minority which was ignored by the school authorities.

'On the one occasion I was a victim,' he said, 'I rationalised it by saying that it was probably my fault anyway, and that I had deserved the "punishment". Telling my parents I had been molested in a shower would have driven a fault line through their unquestioning faith in the integrity of Catholic priests.'

Over the next few days, I received many more messages of support, one of which seemed to hold a vital clue. The message talked about sexual abuse by one of the priests at the school, but did not name him. I replied several times, asking the contact to tell me the priest's name. The contact refused each time saying that he just couldn't face the thought of his family, now grown up like mine, finding out about it. He was desperately sorry, but he just couldn't risk it.

A week went by and I'd heard no more from this man. Then, one afternoon, as I sat at my desk wondering what to do next, 'YOU HAVE E-MAIL' popped up on the screen.

'I've changed my mind,' the message said. 'I will tell you who it was, but you have to promise not to involve me. It was Fr Madden who abused me.' I felt physically sick and my heart began to race. Fr Madden was, of course, the very same priest to whom I had made my confession.

Stephen had made an appointment for us both to meet a barrister who, he had been told, was experienced in dealing with child abuse cases. So, armed with my latest 'clue', off we went to see him. He was not what I had expected. He had little if any understanding of the impact of child-hood sexual abuse on males. He even doubted that the mental breakdown I had suffered recently was in fact PTSD. I was annoyed by his attitude, so I asked him if he had any experience in cases involving psycho-sexual trauma. He was clearly uncomfortable at the question, not because he couldn't give me a positive answer, but simply because I had dared to ask him such a question.

I was not impressed by this man and wanted to leave. The clincher was when he said it would cost about £50,000 to bring a case to court, and in his view, I had a less than 30 per cent chance of success. Even if I did win, the damages would be modest. I thanked him for his time, and we left. On the way home, I told Stephen that I would do it on my own.

'What, act for yourself?'

'Yes. I am just as capable of screwing the case up as he is, but for a fraction of the cost!' We both laughed.

After a brief pause, Stephen said: 'You're serious aren't you?

'You'd better believe it', I replied. 'Deadly, bloody serious.'

The following day was 20 October, my birthday. I was 49 years old. What better day to begin the next stage in my fight for justice? I took a deep breath and plunged right in, writing to the solicitors acting for the school, advising them that I was now acting as litigant in person, and that they should correspond directly with me from now on. I told them that I intended to sue them and Madley, and that I would be filing a claim for damages in the High Court as soon as I had completed the documentation. I also added that I had now received testimonies from two other pupils at my school who stated that they had been sexually abused by Fr Madden. I sent a copy to the headmaster of the school Madley had been moved to, and a copy to the current headmaster of my old school.

Two days later, the school's solicitors replied. It was a very different response to the original dismissive letter they had sent Stephen all those months ago. They asked if I could give them a little more time, but implored me not to think that they were trying to be anything other than very concerned. They took the matter very seriously, but in light of recent developments, they would need to speak in some detail with their client. They also assured me that I should not be concerned if the heads of the two schools did not reply to my letters directly. All correspondence would be dealt with by them. At long last, I had managed to find and press their 'panic' button, so, I wrote to them again, asking for the names and addresses of all involved so I could write to them individually to ask them to provide witness statements. I was not the least bit fearful of them and I certainly was not going to let them intimidate me again.

On 3 November, they replied, asking for yet more time as they were now 'taking instructions on all the issues' I had raised. They again assured me that everyone was taking the matter 'very seriously'. However, unbeknown to me at the time, there were other dark forces at work in the background.

That evening, I logged on to my web site to check the e-mail. The message on my screen said simply: 'ACCESS DENIED'. I tried again. 'ACCESS DENIED'. I sent a quick e-mail to the web site host asking if the system was down.

'We have been ordered to shut down your site,' came the reply.

'By whom?' I asked.

'A teachers' union.'

So, even though I hadn't named him on the site, Madley had gone to his union, the NASUWT, and asked them to protect him. I was now up against a very powerful force. It was time to take the gloves off.

The following morning, I rang the regional office of the union that served the area where Madley had last worked. Eventually, after the usual run-a-round, I was put through to the Regional Director. I asked him if he had shut down my site – 'yes or no?' He wasn't willing at first to tell me anything. I explained a bit more about what Madley had actually done to me and asked him how he would feel if Madley's next victim was his son? Eventually, he confirmed that they had taken the action on behalf of one of their members after receiving a request from the member, who 'has not been charged, let alone convicted, with any offence'. If I wanted to take the matter further, I should write to the union's head office.

That afternoon, I wrote to the then General Secretary of the union, Nigel de Gruchy, asking him why he had shut down my site. He did not reply. I wrote to him several more times, but still got no reply. The union's actions in closing down my web site, coupled with their silence, made me feel abused all over again. It also showed that all those fine words sent to me by the DfEE and the County Council about how they have tightened up their child protection procedures was no more than hot air. I thought back to something the barrister had said to me: 'You could always name him and let him sue you for libel. He probably wouldn't want to though, as it would be far more of a risk for him than it would be for you!'

That was the answer – I would do just that. I contacted my internet service provider and asked if they provided any space on their server for private home pages. Yes, they did. Within hours, everything I had put on my original site was back on the internet! Only this time, I had identified Madley by his full name.

Over the next few days, I e-mailed as many people as I could think of with the web site address asking for anyone who had any information about Madley to contact me. More information came through, although not about Madley specifically, but I passed it all on to the police anyway.

After ten days, Madley's union contacted my internet service provider and threatened them with unspecified action unless they took the site down. However, neither the union nor Madley were threatening any action against me, so the barrister had been right. In a way, I didn't mind now as I'd got more than enough people to look at the site. Everyone who needed to know did know. The site was duly shut down, reluctantly, by the ISP, who told me that they were very sorry to have to close my site, but as it contained material that infringed their own policies, they had no choice. They said that they were doing so with a heavy heart, but wished me luck! Who said the corporate world had no room for people's feelings?

The time had come to concentrate my efforts on the legal case, but with no real knowledge of the law, I was going to have to go back to school. I went to my local library and borrowed all the books they had about civil law and criminal law. I read and read until I could read no more, and by the end of November, I had finished preparing a formal statement of claim using the format shown in the law books. I sent a copy of this to the school's solicitors, with an outline of my case, explaining what I was going to sue their client for, and why.

On 29 November they replied, saying that they had had a meeting with representatives of their client at which they had considered my letters.

'Our client now needs a little more time to consider further some ideas for a constructive approach to resolving the issues you have raised. The purpose of writing at the moment is to assure you that our client has matters under active consideration. We hope to be in a position to come back to you substantively before very much longer, and appreciate your patience.'

It was just over a year since the first, dismissive contact with them. Finally, it looked as though they were going to make a move. I was drained and exhausted, but happy.

Chapter 11

The Reckoning

December has always been a special time of the year in our family. It is a time of giving, renewal, hope and celebration. How apt then, that it was December when the school's solicitors offered their olive branch, spurred on perhaps by the knowledge that I intended to file my claim against them in the High Court any day.

The content of their letter was both unexpected and hard to believe. I read it several times just to be sure I was not dreaming. They said that they had now received instructions from their client and were writing to set out a way forward. Their proposal was for the school and me to try to resolve the issues between us through a process of formal mediation administered by an independent body. They said the mediation process was very simple and very speedy.

'It might be possible to produce an outcome by, say, the end of February. Our client would be represented at the mediation by someone who had authority to enter into a final and binding resolution of the issues between you and the school. We look forward to hearing from you with what we hope will be a positive response.'

I almost went into shock. What they were really saying was that they did not want to get anywhere near a courtroom, preferring to settle the matter out of court. After all this time and energy, the end was in sight. I showed the letter to my wife Barbara, and then to each of my children in turn. They all agreed it would be a good idea to try. I mulled it over for several hours, trying to work out why the school authorities were now so keen to settle the matter. Maybe they had found out that there were other victims, maybe their solicitors had told them I was not going to go away? No matter how hard I thought about it, I couldn't come up with a solution that was anything more than guesswork. There were simply too many different scenarios and possibilities. The only way to find out was to sit down round the table and hear what they had to say, so the following day I faxed them a letter confirming my agreement to the mediation.

From then on, events began to move swiftly. A firm of London-based mediators were appointed and a date for the hearing was fixed for 12 February, 2001. I began to feel very anxious. After all this time, all the denials, all the set backs, suddenly they wanted to talk. Was it a trap? Were they just trying to put more pressure on me in the hope that I would go away?

Over the next few days, my resolve began to harden and I started to write out what I would say on the day, but the more I wrote, the more I realised that I couldn't do it on my own. What if I broke down? What if I just couldn't face it once it got underway? I realised I would have to ask someone I could trust to come with me. I would ask Peter Green, someone I had met along my journey, a kind and intelligent man who knew all about the management of vulnerability.

Peter had become a close friend in a very short space of time. I first met him when I went to work at Ashworth Psychiatric Hospital in 1996. He was the only member of the hospital's senior management whom I had come to trust during those terrible months of the judicial enquiry. He was well aware of what I was going through as, for different reasons, he too was going through his own psychological trauma as a result of the fall-out of the inquiry. It was this mutual bond of understanding between us that had cemented our friendship, but whether he would want to involve himself in even more trauma was something I could not just take for granted, I would have to give him the opportunity to say no without him feeling bad about that.

To my relief, he said yes as soon as I asked him. Immediately I began to feel much more positive and a lot less fearful. Peter had many years of experience working with vulnerable children and adults on both sides of the divide – victims and offenders. He understood every aspect of child protection issues and had little time for those who tried to protect abusers at the expense of their victims. He would prove invaluable.

Over the next couple of weeks, I wrote several times more to the general secretary of Madley's union, Nigel de Gruchy, asking for a response to my previous letters. I got none, but rather than continue to challenge him, I decided to put everything on hold so that my family could enjoy a happy Christmas. It was not until I had shut my study door that I realised just how exhausted I was and how remote I had become from the day-to-day life which was going on around me. The break was a wonderful release from it all and it was for me the best Christmas in many a year.

Once the new year had begun, it was time to get back into the fight. I felt regenerated and fired up for what lay ahead. I spent the next three weeks preparing my case summary for the mediators. When I'd completed it, the time had come to tell my abuser what was about to happen. I'd got his address from a colleague who worked in the press. He had a CD with the complete UK electoral register on it! It took him a matter of seconds to find Madley's address. It was the same house he had taken me to all those years ago.

With a mixture of trepidation and anticipation, I wrote to Madley, telling him in very matter-of-fact terms that I would be meeting representatives from his former employer in February to discuss my claim for damages against them. I added that, depending on the outcome of that meeting, I may agree to drop my claim against the school, but regardless of the outcome, 'I will still file a claim for compensatory, aggravated and exemplary damages against you for the terrible things you did to me when I was a child.' Of all the letters I had written so far, this one was the most satisfying, and I read it out loud to myself several times before I signed it and sealed the envelope.

At the beginning of December, I received a copy of the school's case summary, which had been written by their solicitors. When I'd finished reading it, I knew in my heart that all the words of assurance I had been given over the past months by the Local Authority, the Education Department and Social Services were of little use. In reality, we were no further forward now than we were 30 years ago when I was abused. They had all talked about listening to the child, believing the child, and being able to protect victims of abuse through their better understanding of the issues. In practice, as the school's case summary demonstrated, the reality is that victims still have to prove they were abused before anyone takes any notice. Unless they can do that, they face a very steep hill to climb, and, of course, as the statistics show, many simply can't face the struggle and they end their own lives.

Claiming that they were not in any way responsible for what had happened, they concluded their summary by saying that they would 'listen sympathetically to as much as Mr Wilmer wishes to add in person at the mediation. The School's representatives will then do all they can to work constructively towards a solution which repairs the damage to Mr Wilmer' quality of life, which he claims he suffered. The School will consider whether, in the light of all available information, it would be right to acknowledge in appropriate terms that it did not respond appropriately to matters raised by Mr Wilmer, and whether it can assist Mr Wilmer financially in continuing the process of healing and recovery upon which he has embarked.'

Although I had already written and submitted my case summary, I decided that I had to respond to the crap they had put down as their defence. I wrote back to the mediators and challenged the school's 'position' as forcefully as I could. They were not going to walk over me. I was no longer a frightened child and I didn't care about keeping my story out of the news, on the contrary, I wanted everyone to know exactly what these people had done to me, and no doubt to many others besides.

Two days later, I received a letter from another firm of solicitors, acting on Madley's behalf. With pompous indignation, they threatened 'vigorously to defend any action I might take against their client'. They even went as far as saying that my actions thus far had resulted in their client 'suffering with extreme anxiety and stress which has had an adverse affect on his health'. If I were to sue Madley, they said, 'not only will he defend your action, but will also counter-claim against you in your own action, seeking damages and compensation as well as an order for costs'.

I read the letter over and over. If this was the best he could do to frighten me off, it was a pretty pathetic effort. So, he was suffering from extreme anxiety and stress was he? Good, let me make it even more uncomfortable! I wrote back the same day saying that I was not surprised that their client maintained his denial.

'After all, he is looking at a ten-year custodial sentence if convicted. He is therefore hardly likely to willingly admit to the offence is he?' As for the distress he was claiming to have suffered as a result of my disclosure, well, talk about taking the piss, the cheeky git. I ended my letter by saying perhaps he should have thought a little harder about the possible consequences of his actions before he abused and raped me.

'Spit the bones out of that, you bastard,' I said to myself, as I pushed the letter into the post-box.

Chapter 12

Failed Memories

I didn't sleep at all for the next few nights. A million thoughts kept surging through my mind. I wanted it to be over, but I also wanted it to happen. I had spent the past twelve months, day in, day out, preparing for this moment, but when the day finally came, I felt very exposed and unprepared. Although the hearing was not in a courtroom, it was still me against them. I had to be strong. If I weakened, they would crush me. This was a serious business for everyone; they knew it and I knew it, but, as I would one day find out, they also knew far more than me.

Peter picked me up early in the morning and drove me to the place chosen for the mediation. It was a neutral location, miles from either of us. The week before, I had also asked Stephen if he would join us on the day, just in case they tried to out manoeuvre me with legal arguments that I didn't understand. He was waiting for us when we arrived. I can't tell you just how much strength it gave me to see him there. Once inside, we were shown to a room and asked to wait. Tea and coffee were already in the room. I poured a cup for each of us and we chatted about nothing in particular.

After about ten minutes, a woman in her fifties appeared with a man in his thirties. The woman introduced herself as the mediator, and her colleague as her assistant. She appeared confident and friendly, her colleague more anxious and less talkative. I introduced myself, Peter and Stephen, and, after the usual pleasantries and comments about the weather had been exchanged, she explained that the process we were about to engage in would involve a meeting alone with her first, then a joint meeting, then a break for lunch, and finally, a further joint meeting at which, hopefully, a resolution and agreement would be reached. She also said that during the various sessions, she would refer to each of us by our first names to make the discussions more friendly.

By 11a.m. we had finished our meeting with the mediator. It was now time to meet the other side. I was dreading it. I was about to step back 30 years and look into the eyes of those who'd betrayed me all that time ago. I felt like running away, but I knew I had to go into that room. After all this time, I had brought the school authorities back to the table to ask them: 'Do you believe me now?'

The mediator went in first, followed by Stephen, Peter and then me, rather like a boxer being led into the fight venue by his manager and trainer. At the table sat two priests, one old, the other a little younger. A tall man, their solicitor, sat next to them. The mediator introduced us all to each other and we sat down, on opposite sides of the large, rectangular oak table. Peter had earlier agreed with the mediator that he would present the opening statement on my behalf. The mediator brought the meeting to order and we began.

'Peter,' she said. 'Please would you like to begin with your opening.' Before he could speak, I interjected, politely. 'Could I ask that we begin with a prayer?' There was a stunned silence, then the older priest said: 'Yes. I think that would be a good thing to do.' We lowered our heads and he began to recite the prayer that is perhaps the best-known prayer on the planet, the Lord's Prayer:

'Our Father, who art in heaven. Hallowed be thy name. Thy Kingdom come. Thy will be done on earth as it is in heaven. Give us this day our daily bread and forgive us our trespasses as we forgive those who trespass against us. Lead us not into temptation but deliver us from evil, for thine is the kingdom, the power and the glory, for ever and ever. Amen.' It was, in every sense, the only prayer he could have said. When it was finished, Peter picked up his piece of paper and began to speak.

'Gentlemen, my name is Peter Green. I am a close friend of Graham and his family, yet I have known him for just four years. In that relatively short time, however, I have come to know him very well. In 1996, Graham was employed by my Chief Executive to advise the Board of our hospital in relation to a number of highly sensitive issues that were about to be brought into the media spotlight. His experience in media relations was extremely helpful to us, so much so, that, a year later, when we were faced with an inquiry into allegations of child abuse and other issues, he stayed on under my direct supervision as a trusted member of our team.

'It was as a result of the challenges and pressures we faced together in carrying out this difficult and harrowing task that we developed a very close professional bond based on trust, mutual respect and understanding of the issues involved, and it was as a result of this bond that Graham turned to me for help as a friend when, in 1998, his own difficulties began to overwhelm him. It is as his friend that I appear here before you today to speak on his behalf.

'We have all read Graham's case summary and I do not therefore propose to go over it again in any detail. However, what I do want to do is offer some observations and thoughts for consideration as we conduct this process of mediation in an attempt to settle this matter to the benefit of all parties.

'Firstly, let me address the issue of the truth and credibility of children and young people. In my experience as a social worker dealing with the many damaged, abused and betrayed children, young people and adults that I have worked with over the years, I can say without hesitation that when a child or a young person in crisis tells you that they are being abused, they are invariably telling the truth.

'When Graham confessed to Fr Madden, back in the autumn of 1967, he was only just 16 – a minor; frightened, confused and clearly in crisis. Just thinking about the mental anguish he must have gone through in making the decision to disclose what was happening to him is made all the worse when we consider that he did not do it to cause trouble. He did not do it out of spite or a misguided sense of vengeance. He did not do it to empower himself in the eyes of his peers. He did it because he wanted to spare the family of his friend Martin the pain of watching him refuse to take Holy Communion with them at Martin's requiem mass. This act of sacrifice was a remarkable thing for anyone to have done, but especially so a child under the pressures he was facing.

'The circumstances of Graham's disclosure, however, I find deeply disturbing. As I understand things, the sacrament of confession is a central pillar of the Roman Catholic faith. The absolute and guaranteed secrecy of the confessional is the one constant that has not changed since the Catholic Church began. Yet in this case, Graham's secrets were not kept secret, and, if that were not bad enough, they were then used against him by the school. Given that there was no positive outcome for Graham from all this, it is difficult to come up with any justification for Fr Madden's actions at the time of the confession, or the headmaster's subsequent actions when he was also told the details of Graham's confession.

'More recently, however, another former pupil at the school has come forward and said that he and two other boys were "sexually molested" by Fr Madden in the shower after a cross-country run. They were all only 13 years old at the time. Another former pupil has testified that he was physically assaulted by Fr Madden and threatened with a piece of broken plastic rail. These reports paint a very disturbing picture, but, unfortunately, Fr Madden is, of course, no longer with us, so we can't ask him to justify his actions. The headmaster is still alive, however, and we can certainly ask him to justify the actions he took when he was informed after Graham made his first disclosure.

'There is no doubt in my mind that Graham was telling the truth then, and is telling the truth now. But we need not take my word alone on this. The police interviewed Graham at length before they traced, arrested and subsequently interviewed Hugh Madley. They believed Graham at the outset, and they continued to believe him despite the categorical denial made by Mr Madley when they questioned him about Graham's statement – a statement taken during nearly five hours of detailed police interview conducted by trained child protection officers. The Crown Prosecution also believed Graham. When they wrote to him explaining why they could not prosecute without further corroborating evidence, they did not say 'the allegations you made', they said 'the offences committed against you'.

'Graham has also undergone detailed clinical, psychiatric and psychological assessment over the past twelve months by qualified clinicians and therapists, all of whom came to the same, unequivocal conclusion – that Graham had been sexually and psychologically abused as a child, and the impact on him and his development was, and has continued to be, profoundly damaging. The fact that he learnt to cope with the early effects of the abuse and get on with his life as best he could is a testimony to his courage and to the strength of his character, and it is this that brings me to my second point.

'In 1963, Graham was welcomed into the school as a child of twelve, with all of the promise, wonder and potential that lay before him as his mind developed under the staff's care and tuition. He came having worked hard at his primary school where he was assessed under the LEA's five-point scale of assessment as being in the 25 per cent who were above average ability. He also came having shown himself to be a warm and thoughtful child, mindful of others and interested in the world about him. His primary school headmaster, Leonard Cowie, who went on to become a highly respected figure in the educational system, said of him at the time: "It has been a continuous pleasure to have had Graham in the school. We wish him well in his future school life and career."

'And so it was that Graham indeed began to show promise and develop further. For the first three years with you his school reports provide the evidence that he was a good pupil. His conduct in that period was described as "excellent" and his headmaster, wrote in the second year "Graham is making very good progress." How, then, was it that this child – for let us not forget that "child" is what he still was – became a victim of a predatory paedophile – for that is what happened – while he was under your protection? How was it, then, that when, under the most frightening conditions imaginable, this child came to you for help, you failed him? You failed him, not just in your responsibility for his education, but in your responsibility for his physical, emotional and spiritual well-being.

'For any school to have acted in this way is quite simply totally unacceptable. It is so now, and it was so then. The fact that the School is a Roman Catholic school makes it not only totally unacceptable, but absolutely unforgivable. Yet, despite this, Graham has told me that he has forgiven you for your failure. What he cannot do, however, is forget, which is understandable. You cannot change the past, but you can change the future. What you should do now is acknowledge what happened, accept that you failed, apologise and learn the lessons. Only then can Graham move on. Thank you.'

A deafening silence filled the room. It seemed to last for a long time. The mediator looked towards me and asked if I wanted to add anything? I took a deep breath and began to speak.

'This has been a very long journey for me, but it is a journey I have to complete. I owe it to Martin, whose death released me from the night-mare, and I owe it to all of the other victims of abuse whose lives, like mine, will have been blighted by Hugh Madley, but who are still too terrified to speak out about the suffering they have undergone because of this cowardly man.'

I paused for a moment, trying hard to fight the emotion surging within me. I really did try, but I couldn't stop it. The hidden pain was finally out and it totally overwhelmed me. The tears rolled down my face and I began to sob. The child inside me that I had protected for all these years was now here again, right there in front of them. The looks on their faces told me they knew that. I continued to speak, the tears still streaming down my face, but my mind became clearer and I felt an inner calm begin to descend upon me. Gradually, that calm grew stronger and I stopped crying, but not speaking. I took them through every aspect of what it's like to be abused and why they must learn from what happened so they don't repeat their mistakes when the next child comes to them and discloses that they are being abused. I finished by saying that just because they have signed up to the latest 'child protection' policies, that does not mean all the paedophiles have gone away.

After a further pause, the older priest began to speak in a decidedly shaky voice.

'I was appointed headmaster of your school just after you left. I knew nothing of what you have told us, and nor, I fear, do any of the other members of the Salesian Order. We only have your word for what you say happened, but it is clear that something may have happened. What I would say to you Graham is that you did not do anything wrong. If what you say happened did happen, then you are not guilty of anything.'

Although I could hear his words very clearly, I could not believe what he was saying. It was as if he was trying to address me from the position of the priest, as the confessor, to me, as the penitent. I knew then that I was in the presence of people who lived in a very different world, and had very different values. As far as they were concerned, no matter what I or anyone else said, they were still denying any knowledge of what I had told them all those years ago, and was now telling them again.

I sat and listened as the two priests and the lawyer then took it in turn to speak on different aspects of the six objectives I had challenged them with. Explanations and assurances, references and testimonials; they had come equipped with all the evidence they could muster to make the point that what I was claiming had happened to me could not happen again, at least not at their school. When they had finished, they looked pleased with their work, as if they had sorted it all out. I felt shattered and very emotional. 'Judgement Day', as it was supposed to have been, was not turning out as I had prayed, and it was taking its toll on me. I looked over at Peter and Stephen. The look of disbelief on their faces was in stark contrast to the smug smiles of the two priests. We broke for lunch.

After lunch, which the two priests had tucked into with relish, seemingly unmoved by the morning's events, the situation began to change when the subject of compensation was on the table. Stephen asked for a private meeting with their lawyer, and the two of them went off into another room. Eventually they returned, having been unable to agree on a figure, so we were sent back to our room. After about 20 minutes, the mediator came to see us. She looked nervous. She began to go back over the day's proceedings and talk about the importance of me being able to draw a line under the events of the past and move on. She clearly had no idea about the real impact of sexual abuse on children.

Stephen, now showing signs of irritation with the woman, interrupted her and asked if they were going to make an offer or not. She paused for a moment and then said: 'Twenty thousands pounds – that's all they can offer.' Her words hung in the air like blue smoke.

'That's ridiculous,' Stephen said. 'Their legal fees will be more than that.' He turned to me and asked what I thought?

'It's not an apology – it's just a token payment, presumably to shut me up again. I want an apology, with no strings attached. You can go back and tell them that I don't accept their miserable offer and they should be ashamed.' I got up and left the room, followed a few moments later by Peter and Stephen. Once outside, Peter asked me if I was O.K. I said I was angry and needed time to think. We said goodbye and Peter drove me home. I felt humiliated, but not crushed. My mind was spinning and I desperately wanted to go to sleep; it was the only way I was going to shut out all of the emotions whirling round in my head like a tornado. I told Barbara and the children what had happened. They found it hard to understand, but told me not to worry. I went to bed and slept the sleep of the dead.

For the next two days, I sat in my study listening to music and staring out of the window. On the third day, I began to focus on what had happened. I went through in my head the fundamentals of why I had gone back to challenge them. Gradually, it dawned on me that I had been distracted by the compensation issue. The money wasn't what it was all about. The amount was irrelevant – what I had wanted was something from them that proved I had gone back, faced them down and forced them to put their hands in their miserable, grubby little pockets, hand over some cash to say 'sorry'.

The more I thought about it, the more I knew in my heart that I was right; holding out for a better offer was not on my agenda, and never had been. I rang the school's solicitor and explained my thinking. We talked for about half an hour, at the end of which we agreed that I would accept their offer, and that would be an end of the matter. I had achieved part of what I'd set out to do, even if they had not admitted their guilt, nor said sorry. In my mind – confused as it was – I needed something to show that I had looked them square in the eyes and come away with my head held high and my dignity restored, even if, in reality, I was still tilting at windmills.

Two days later, he telephoned me and read out a draft agreement. It was pretty much as I had thought it would be – the Salesians will give you the cash; you say nothing about it to anyone; and no one will be any the wiser. There was, however, one other condition I had not expected; they wanted me to withdraw the complaint I had made to the police. I was almost speechless – after all they had said in that room about how their new child protection policies enshrined the importance of not pro-tecting abusers, that was exactly what they were still attempting to do. The spots on the leopard had clearly not changed as much as they had assured me they had.

After a short pause to gather my composure, I told him that by making such a request he was in serious danger of undoing all that had been achieved between us. I felt a growing sense of anger inside but, as I now had all the power, there was nothing to be gained from ranting on at him further, so I explained in the calmest voice I could that to withdraw my complaint would be to turn my back on all the other victims that I knew were still out there, too frightened to come forward and disclose their awful secrets. 'Under no circumstances would I betray them.'

He got the message loud and clear, mumbled an apology of sorts and said that it was his job to ask me, but I should not read into his question that this was what the school authorities had wanted. Even though I felt from his tone that he not being straight with me, I said that I would forget he had asked. He gave a detectable sigh of relief and then said he would write to me shortly to finalise the agreement.

About a week later, a letter arrived from the school's solicitors, containing a cheque for £20,000, and the signed agreement, which stated that, in return for their hush money, I would not sue them for any act of negligence on their part, and that I would not mention them, or my former teacher, in anything I wrote or said about my experiences. They now considered the matter closed.

This part of my struggle was over but, the 'matter' was far from closed. They had silenced the child, but they cannot silence the man. It was, after all, Fr Madden who told me during my confession that it was my conscience that had led me to the right path.

'Always follow your conscience,' he had told me, 'and in God's eyes you will not be found wanting.' The vulnerable little boy inside me that I had protected for all these years could now rest in peace, but the man that child had become still had work to do. I would find a way to bring Madley to account, and I would find his other victims, and release them too.

Chapter 13

Dead Man Walking

As the days that followed blended themselves together, I felt more and more that I had still not brought closure to everything that had happened. I was still receiving treatment and counselling. I was still broke, having used all of the £20,000 from the school to pay off some of my debts. I had no work and no real prospects that I could see in the near term. But I had learned so much about myself in the process I had been through, and I had received so much love and support from Barbara, our children and so many others during my struggle. Surely there must be a way of making something worthwhile come out of it?

The more I thought about it, the more I began to realise that my salvation lay not in walking away from the past, but in embracing it so that others could benefit. I asked myself what I had really achieved from my struggle. Did I get the justice I wanted so desperately? Did I bring my abuser to book? And why did I blame him so much when other men had abused me as well? Why hadn't I challenged them too? Have I really made the journey from victim to survivor, or am I still walking along the road, kicking boulders as I go, angry and frustrated, blaming everyone else for the problems I had suffered? What exactly have I learned from my experiences, and what should I do next? The answer to these and many other such questions was in truth that I did not really know. The only way I was going to sort it all out was to write it all down.

It took me many more months to find the strength to sit down and begin to write my story, 'Survivor', which was eventually published in September 2004, as the thought of going through it all again was hard to face. But, once I had begun, I could not stop. I knew as I wrote that one day, other victims who needed to release themselves from the pain they carried, but did not know where to start, would be able to read my story and find the strength within themselves to begin the journey out of the darkness and into the light.

What no-one knew, of course, least of all me, was that my story was far from over. But, for now, there were many more questions I would have to answer before I could finish the story at I knew it then, for example, had I really forgiven those who trespassed against me, or was I just saying that? It has taken me a long time to sort that out, but, at the time, I concluded that Madley, and the other men who abused me, would still have to answer for their actions. It was not my responsibility to judge them, nor should I have to. But I could, and should, forgive them. I argued that unless I could find it in my heart to forgive them, I couldn't honestly say that I am a survivor? No, I would still be a victim. So, the way I came to terms with this dilemma was by accepting that, although Madley and others caused me great harm, they had also, unwittingly, given me a first-hand understanding of how paedophiles work; the damage they do to their young victims, and how that damage manifests itself as their victims grow into adults. Having used this understanding in my own recovery, I knew that I could also use it to help others recover. So, I said to myself, I am able to forgive them because they gave me such a comprehensive set of unique and powerful tools that I could not have got any other way. It was a useful argument at the time, but, as I was to discover, it was paper thin. There still lay in me so much anger and pain waiting to emerge, and emerge it would. In the meantime, I continued to address such issues in my writing as, what had all this done to my religious faith?

The answer was that it destroyed my faith in the Roman Catholic Church, and it destroyed my trust in people in authority. When I took communion at Martin's funeral mass, it was the last time I would take it for many years to come. I hated the clergy, absolutely and completely. To me, the priests were not 'men of God', but corrupt, abusive, lying, evil 'men of men', and I wanted no part in their church of catastrophe; and that meant all churches, not just the Roman Catholic Church.

But the years of indoctrination had made their mark on me. It was not quite so easy to turn my back on the Church in the way I had wanted to. I continued to suffer from the awful fear of punishment the priests at school had instilled in me as a child, and for years, I felt unwanted, alone and valueless. My soul was dead. I felt no real emotion within me, I just pretended to the outside world that I was normal, happy and full of life.

As the years went by, though, I became less scornful and over time I developed my own bond with God. I had never been far from God and I found it easy to pray to the God I believed in, who was a God who loved those who could not defend themselves, not a God who sent you to hell for all eternity if you died in a state of mortal sin – sins such as missing Easter Mass, using contraceptives and taking Communion without going to confession first. How ridiculous is that? Jesus didn't say at the Last Supper: 'Don't do this in memory of me unless you have first gone to see a priest and confessed your wicked sins.' No, far from it, he just said: 'Do this in memory of me.'

I still wanted to be close to God, so I created my own religion, not based on churches or purple robes or confession or mass or dogmas, or on any of the rest of the nonsense that was how I saw the human made religions of the world. I created a religion based simply on asking God to help others who were in trouble. It went like this: if I saw someone who had broken down on the motorway, or fallen over in the street, or who looked in need of someone to help them, or even love them, I would say a simple prayer: 'Dear God, please help them.' Five words – my religion was based on just five words, and it worked. It kept me close to God and helped me feel some sense of value and purpose, however small.

When Barbara came into my life, I was, at first, scornful of her religion too. She had been brought up in the Methodist Church. In fact, her father was a Methodist minister, a man I grew to love and respect greatly. Her mother was quite simply a saint, and when she died, a great hole opened in our lives. She had been so wonderful to me and our three children when they were young that her loss was a terrible blow to us all. But I have often felt her guiding hand since she died and I know that she sits close to God. I hope and pray that I will one day see her again so I can thank her for everything she did for me.

Barbara's faith is strong, but it is not a faith in any particular Church or religious institution. She believes, as indeed do I, that all human beings have the intrinsic ability to cause suffering to others, but we are not pro-grammed to do that. We have the choice, as we all have an instinctive understanding of the difference between good and bad. At the end of the day, it is all about how you choose to live your life. She said to me once, if you really want to understand the nature of the choice we have, read the sermon on the mount.

I did, and it moved me in a way I had not experienced before; its logic is so simple, so moving, so beautiful. Barbara is a primary school teacher. She teaches children in a very deprived area in north west England. I see her practise her faith in the way she teaches those young people. She is so patient and caring with them; an inspiration to me and all those around her.

The months that followed seemed to blend into each other as life began to get back to something more normal, or at least that is what I thought was happening. In June 2000, we had moved to New Brighton, a wonderful coastal town on the tip of the Wirral Peninsular, with acres of sandy beaches that stretch for miles when the tide is out. I was still not well enough to go back to work, but I felt much stronger and, foolishly, I stopped taking the anti-depressants I had been swallowing every day for the past two years.

The effect was unnoticeable at first. Then, one morning, as I walked along the beach with my faithful dog Emma, I began to cry. It came from somewhere deep inside me, a feeling of total hopelessness and despair. It was a blackness I had never known before, and it completely took me over. After some twenty minutes or so, it passed and I walked home with Emma. She knew – the way she looked at me told me she could sense something was wrong.

Over the next few weeks, the blackness darkened even further. I began to spend hours at a time standing on the shoreline, staring out across the Irish Sea. I felt numb, useless and so desperately lonely. I said nothing to Barbara as I was not really sure what was happening to me, but that all changed on the day I began composing my suicide note to my family. As I walked along the beach, reading it out to myself in my head, I felt a wonderful sense of peace. They would understand. I was of no use to them anyway. It would all soon be over. All I had to do was keep walking – into the water, and then to sleep; at last I would be able to sleep. No more nightmares, no more pain, no more confusion, no more excuses. Then Eve appeared; my daughter's face – as clear as if she were standing in front of me. 'You can't leave us,' she said. 'You just can't.' It was over in a flash. I threw myself onto the beach and sobbed, digging my fingers into the sand as if clinging to life itself, which was exactly what I was doing.

That evening, I went to see Dr Dolan and told her what had happened. She told me I had been lucky. 'Most people don't stop when they reach the point you were about to cross.' We argued for the next five minutes over why I did not need to be admitted to a psychiatric ward for my own safety. She was insistent that she had a duty of care to protect me. I was terrified at the prospect and, only after agreeing to phone her every day for the next two weeks to report my feelings, did she relent! She prescribed Seroxat antidepressants and I made my way home, still confused, but very much wanting to stay alive. I was now more determined than ever to find a way to bring those bastards to account. I would not let them take me away from those I loved so dearly. My resolve was restored, but I was in a much poorer state of mental health than I realised. It would be three more years before I finally found the key that released me from the nightmare.

Chapter 14

David

I have never believed that our lives are predetermined by some higher authority. Destiny is not something that is set in stone. We have choice, and it is the choices we make that determine the outcome of our successes, our failures and our ultimate fate. What we have no control over, until they have happened, are the events that occur as we make our way along the paths we choose. Nor can we know in advance who we will meet on the journey and how they will change our lives, and we theirs. And so it was with David.

Not long after we moved to New Brighton, I bought a boat, an ex-customs launch called Kittiwake. I had discovered her on the internet, languishing in a boat yard in Swansea, and she was very cheap. It was love at first site. She was fifty years old, thirty-two feet long and so beautiful. She was also in need of considerable repair, but I knew nothing much about boats – except that I wanted one with a passion! What I had not fully appreciated was that, in a maritime environment such as New Brighton, boats, regardless of their shape, size, age, history or future, fuelled the same passion in others, and I was soon befriended by the most wonderful group of men who had, between them, all the knowledge there was to have about boats – how they were made, how they worked, how to look after them, how to navigate them and, most important of all – how to stay safe on them! They knew everything there was to know about the sea, its perils, its joy and its wonder, all of which they combined into one simple rule: 'you can learn to love the sea, but it will never love you. If you want to stay alive – remember that.'

With their help, Kittiwake was brought to Birkenhead on a lorry,

lowered into Alfred Dock by crane and towed to her mooring alongside
the retired submarine HMS Onyx. Over the next few months, she was
lovingly restored to her former glory by my new friends, who by now
had become so much a part of our family, it was as if we had known
them for ever. It was a joyous experience to spend time with them, listening to their stories, watching and learning from their skills, and feeling
the inner warmth that flows from enthusiasm combined with genuine
friendship. These were real men; hard men on the outside, forged from
years of military service and decades at sea. Yet they were still capable
of expressing their humanity, their emotions and their fears, if only you
would let them.

Although I had come to know him quite well, the bond I forged with
David began unexpectedly on a cold winter morning. Kittiwake was now
moored permanently in the River Mersey, between New Brighton and
Egremont. It was late November and the coddling had just arrived in the
river. The rest of the crew had been on the boat all night fishing. David and
I had planned to join them in the morning, but when we tied up alongside
in the dinghy, the boat was empty. They had obviously had enough of the
cold and gone home early to get warm, eat and then sleep.

We climbed aboard, tied up the dinghy and checked the boat over,
hoping to find the kettle still warm. Not only was it freezing cold, but
the others had taken the matches with them. As neither of us smoked,
we had no way to light the stove, and the thought of going ashore to get
a light was too much trouble.

'We'll just have to drink wine then,' David stated with assurance.

'We don't have any,' I replied.

'Correction,' said David. 'You don't have any!'

He disappeared forward, emerging a few moments later clutching a
wooden box from which he took out six bottles of red wine

'Jacob's Creek Special Reserve,' he said in triumph. 'I put it on the
boat some time ago – just in case!'

By the time it had got dark, not only had we drunk all the wine, we
had also told each other about many of the dark and sinister memories
we each carried, but not all. Nevertheless, in the space of the time it had
taken for the tide beneath us to ebb, and then flood again, I had shared my
secrets with this man as if he were my brother. In the months that were to
follow, I would come to know him even better as, although we could not
have known it then, we were going to travel along the same road together
for some time to come. It would be a journey of discovery for both of us,
not all of which would be happy, and much of which would challenge us
beyond the scope of anything either of us knew then.

A few weeks later, Kittiwake was lost in a violent storm that made the river boil as if in were in a terrible rage. It is not uncommon for storms to erupt from nowhere in Liverpool bay at that time of year, but the ferocity of this particular one, which combined the power of force ten winds and a large spring tide, caught us all by surprise. Fortunately there was no one on the boat when she broke free from her mooring and headed up river at speed, capsizing not far from the Liver building on the world famous Liverpool water front. At least she sank in a noble place!

Once the shock of losing our pride and joy had passed, David and I began to talk more about another project I had been thinking about for some time now – to set up a charity to help adult male victims of child abuse, most of whom, like me, found life hard to cope with when they reached the age of 40. The evidence showed that males who have been sexually abused as children carry a self-destruct button, which remains in-operative until triggered by some other traumatic event later in their lives, often with catastrophic consequences for themselves and those around them, as I had experienced so vividly for myself. The key to keeping such men from going off the rails was to allow them to talk openly about their past in an atmosphere of understanding and support, but finding such places was like looking for the lost city of Atlantis.

My plan was to set up just such an organisation, using the power of the internet, to link survivors together, and create an electronic library of all the current thinking about child abuse, its impact and how to cope with its awful legacy. My problem was that I knew I could not do it on my own – I just didn't have the energy, but with David's help, the pos-sibility of creating a male survivors support group seemed much more achievable.

What made David special was that he was fearless – nothing seemed to daunt him. Five tours of duty in Northern Ireland, combat in the Falklands and months of special operations in Colombia and other such murky places made this former marine a force to be reckoned with. He was very definitely the person you wanted standing next to you in a pub fight, yet he had also had immense depth and compassion, as I would soon discover. He also had a secret that he had not shared with me that day on the boat. It would a while yet before he would tell me, but when he did, it would cement our relationship so strongly that we would become inseparable, and, at the age of 52, I would finally know what it was like to have a brother.

By the end of March 2003, we had created the web site and set up the charity, which we called The Lantern Project. Twelve months later, we had made contact with some 20,000 people from all over the world, all wanting help and information about child abuse. The scale of the response was staggering, and it has continued to grow to this day, with more than

70,000 people now using the web site on a continuous basis.

It was another twelve months before David told me his secret, although by then I had pretty much worked it out for myself. When he did finally sit me down and tell me that he too had been sexually abused as a child, it still came as a terrible shock, yet it also brought to the surface a deeper understanding between us that will never leave me, and which I will always be grateful for.

Chapter 15

Angels Passing Through

Eight months before I set up the Lantern Project, two 10 year old school-girls, Holly Wells and Jessica Chapman, vanished from their homes in Soham, Cambridgeshire. Their bodies were found in a ditch thirteen days later on 17 August 2002, after one of the biggest police operations ever mounted in the UK. On 17 December, 2003, sixteen months later, to the day, Ian Huntley, a school caretaker, already known to the police as a child sex offender, was convicted at the Old Bailey in London of their murder and sentenced to two life terms in prison.

Two days later, the then Home Secretary, announced an independent inquiry into the way the police had handled the previous allegations of sexual abuse made against Huntley by other young children, none of which had ended in a conviction. The inquiry, unprecedented in British legal history, concluded that it was not safe to ignore allegations of sexual abuse simply because they had not resulted in a trial or prosecution. Major changes were then made to the way such allegations would be recorded in the future, and a new public body was established to take over the responsibility for collating such information from the police.

Barbara and I had followed the tragic story of Holly and Jessica since they went missing, so it was with a strong sense of significance when she arrived home from shopping one day with two stone angels.

'I saw these and thought we should place them in the garden in memory of Holly and Jessica.' She took a while placing them in the corners of our courtyard among the pots of fragrant herbs and colourful geraniums. 'They will be safe here,' she said. We held hands and just stood there looking at the two little angels, and we both cried. I felt very sad and I could feel the anger growing within me. Holly and Jessica had been killed because everyone who could have done something to prevent it chose not to. If only the police had listened more carefully to the allegations made by other children against Huntley, it would never have happened. It then came to me as I looked at the two statues – that was the answer – I would make a new allegation against Madley, and this time, they would have to record it on the national police computer. That way, at least I could ensure that Madley would never be able to work with children again in a school. Under the new system, my allegation would pop up when anyone carried out a check with the Criminal Records Bureau, now mandatory for all organisations employing people to work with children and vulnerable people.

It took me a while to put together my strategy. I knew I would face considerable resistance from the Salesians if I did anything that directly contravened the agreement I had signed with them. What I had to avoid at all costs was an injunction preventing me from doing or saying anything about what had happened. Eventually, I decided that the best option was to back them into a corner by the force of argument, as they had already shown that they were not the sharpest tools in the box. The first step was to re-open the dialogue with the Salesians' lawyers to see how they would react to me poking around once more in the file they had told me back in 2001 was finally 'closed'.

Their initial reaction was blunt and uncompromising, and totally predictable. Under no circumstances would the Salesians be prepared to discuss the case with me. As far as they were concerned, the matter was 'dead and buried'. I responded by suggesting to them that times had changed over the past couple of years, and there was still the possibility that Madley could offend again. Their reaction, which took a while, was less hostile, but the Salesians were still of the opinion that the past, whatever that was, was now 'firmly behind' me. They were clear that they felt no obligation or need to look at the case any further. Their lawyer, however, in a rare example of a lawyer showing a human face, added that he thought I should at least seek my own legal advice, given the 'strength of your feelings, which the Order does acknowledge.'

So, then, a weakness in their position was apparent, even if only in the form of a throw away line by their lawyer, but it was all I needed. Someone once told me that if you are going to hunt elephants – take a big gun. I responded with as much ferocity as I could muster without seeming as if I had simply lost the plot and was just venting my anger once more. 'You should consider the damage that the Order would suffer if Madley were to re-offend, and it came out that they had refused me leave to try to stop that happening, when they knew in their hearts that it was possible – even if they still maintained that they had only my word for what had happened.' I knew that in the current climate, with the Roman Catholic Church around the world still reeling from the flood of criminal and civil prosecutions taking place, following the decades of child abuse by priests they had covered up that was now, finally, emerging into the public domain, to the shock, horror and absolute disbelief of just about everyone, Christians and non Christians alike, this thought would put them between a rock and a hard place.

To my complete amazement, it worked! On 10 February, 2004, their lawyers responded, saying that, having re-considered the matter, the Order would 'under no circumstances want any individual who had engaged in child abuse to be free to do so again.' Accordingly, they would not enforce the agreement we had made were I to begin steps to bring a private criminal prosecution against Madley, which is the course of action I had suggested to them would be the way forward to ensure he could be stopped from posing a risk to children in the future. But they were still in denial, adding: 'You will understand, in the context, that this is a general statement of principle, and is not to be taken as a specific reference to Mr Madley as to whose activities the Order has no information other than that which you have supplied'. At the time, I paid little attention to this, as it was what they had always said. It would prove to be their undoing; another throwaway line by a lawyer that probably seemed innocent enough to him at the time, but it would come to haunt them all when the final count was made.

Over the next three weeks, I corresponded several times with Surrey Police, reviewing the previous investigation and seeking their advice as to the possible course of action now open as a result of the Salesians' change of position. After taking their own legal advice, the police said they were prepared to proceed with a private criminal prosecution, although they were adamant that I was facing a very steep hill. They did confirm though that were I to instruct them to go ahead, my allegations would indeed be recorded on the police national computer, and with the newly formed Criminal Records Bureau. 'What you will need to do to begin the process is to write to Mr Madley and inform him of your instructions to us. We will then interview him and take it from there'. I was almost beside myself with joy. I had done it – well, I had breathed life back into the case, and I had a second chance. I would not let them escape twice, but I wondered if I really had the strength to see it through, something that played on my mind for the next few weeks, creating new nightmares and flashbacks, but I had become used to those now, so on I struggled, buoyed up by a new sense of purpose, and supported by my long-suffering wife Barbara and our three children, all of whom had come to terms with the fact that I was never going to give up until I had put a stop to Madley's potential to destroy the lives of other children.

Chapter 16

The Truth Emerges

As the cold winds of March gave way to spring, the cycle of life all around us continued its relentless journey onwards. Flower buds appeared in the hawthorn tree, the swallows, swifts and martins arrived from Africa, filling the skies over New Brighton once more with aerial displays that brought joy to my heart. I was filled with a new sense of purpose, and I felt deep down that I could walk the last part of this long, dark journey with the same courage and fortitude that nature was showing me was possible, as long as I did not give up.

On April Fools' Day, 2004, I sat down and wrote once more to the man who had terrorised me for so much of my life. I told him in un-emotional language that I had now embarked on a course that would only end when the truth was finally out. I explained that the Salesians had given me their pledge that they would not stand in my way, and that it was now evident that they had some doubt as to his innocence. I spelt out in exact terms what it was that I was hoping to achieve, and that I would never stop until I had brought him to justice. It was a difficult letter to write, but not because I couldn't find the right words, it was more that I felt naked again by being in such close contact with this evil little man. The only consolation I could draw from it was knowing that this single page of text would cause him alarm, insecurity and fear. Good; let it begin, I thought, as I sealed the envelope and walked down the hill to the post office near the sea front. This was a letter that needed to be sent first class, recorded and with conviction. It was not a long letter, but it would prove to be the most important I had ever written, and I had written a few over the past five years!

Five days later, a small, cream-coloured envelope dropped through our letterbox, landing face-up on the doormat. It was hand written and I recognised the writing instantly. I picked it up and took it into my study. Barbara had already left for school. I was alone in the house, except for Timmy, our beautiful greyhound. We had got him from a rescue centre three months earlier, after dear old Emma had passed on to chase God's sheep across the heavens. Timmy looked much better now than he had done when we went to collect him. Such is the wonder of these incredible animals; they suffer horrendous abuse at the hands of humans, yet they bear no grudge. With love and care, they recover, and in time, learn to trust again, as if nothing bad had ever happened.

He could sense my anticipation as I turned the envelope over and over in my hands. Only hours ago, this letter had been in Madley's hands. The same hands that had done me so much harm all those years ago. It was not what I had expected. I had steeled myself for another indignant reply from his solicitor, threatening me with boiling oil and other such torments if I continued to make these 'outrageous allegations' against their client. I sat down on the settee. Timmy jumped up beside me and looked at me with pricked ears. 'It's alright,' I said. 'I've been waiting for this for a long time now. Let's see what the bastard has to say for himself.'

I opened the envelope carefully with the silver paper knife Peter had given me at his daughter's christening the year before, half praying that somehow, using the knife would make the contents more bearable. Inside was a single piece of notepaper, on which were seven short lines of neat handwriting. 'Dear Graham, I wonder if you would be prepared to meet me some time in the near future? I hope you are well. I do not have your phone number, but here is mine if you wish to speak to me to make arrangements. Yours sincerely, Hugh. PS. I have an answer phone if I am out.' I read the words again and again, trying to understand what this was all about. My mind went blank. It was as if he was standing right there in front of me. I felt a cold panic descend on me and the tears began to flow. Timmy licked my face. I felt his warm breath and put my arms around his long neck, dropping the letter on the floor. Now it was his turn to rescue me!

Gradually, as we sat their together, a feeling of calm began to flow through me once more. I picked up the letter, put it back into the envelope and rang David.

'Stay where you are. I'm on my way round.'

His voice was reassuring and added to my sense of calm. It would be OK. He would know what to do.

'I hope you are well?', said David, as he read the letter with a look of disbelief on his face.

'The cheeky bastard! After everything he has done, and all this time? Talk about taking the piss.'

'What do you think he is after?', I asked.

'He wants to make a deal – offer you some cash to make you drop the case, or something like that.'

'I don't want to make a deal. I want him to fry.'

'Well, then let's fry him,' said David.

'How?'

'Write back and say you don't want to see him, but you are prepared to listen to what he has to say. Would you ring him?'

'I don't think I could face that,' I said. The thought of his voice again. No, I can't do that yet.'

I could feel my heart beating against my chest. I wanted to cry again. David could see my distress. He walked over to me and put his arms around me. My brother was here and he would take care of me.

'Listen mate. We will get through this. He won't hurt you anymore. I won't let him.'

I dried my eyes and sat down at the computer.

'O.K., let's see which of us is in control now.'

Twenty minutes later, after several attempts at a suitable reply, we agreed the contents of my response. It said, simply, that I had discussed his letter with my counsellor, and that I was not ready to meet him, but that I would correspond with him, so would he like to tell me why he wants to meet with me after all this time? I posted the letter and waited.

Two days later, another cream-coloured envelope dropped through my letter box. The speed of Madley's reply; good old-fashioned return of post, rang alarm bells in my head. Was I falling into a trap of some kind? Two letters in less than a week from a man who, not so long ago, could not remember anything when interviewed by the police about me. I put the unopened letter on my desk and walked into the garden for a while to give me time to calm down. I was feeling very anxious; a cold panic began to fill my head. I had only just begun my contact with him, yet already he seemed to be taking control. After a while, I went back into the study and opened the letter. I read it carefully, then read it again. The same line jumped out at me each time: 'One thing I have realised is that I accidentally misled you in 68. We were talking but were interrupted. I did not complete what I was saying to you and I believe this caused you grief.'

Try as I could, I could not understand what on earth this meant. Talking? Talking about what, and when? How did he mislead me? I phoned David who came over immediately and read the letter, almost snatching it out of my hand in his haste to see for himself what Madley had said.

'He's a cunning animal, this Madley, but so are we. I think we can get the bastard now,' David said with a mixture of contempt and excitement in his voice.

'How do we do that, then?'

'Write back, and say that your counsellor – me – would be happy to talk to him to see what he wants to say to you. Give him some dates and times; make it look like you are trying to be as helpful as possible. This guy is arrogant – he will love the fact that you are compliant once more with his wishes – he loves to be in control.'

I was not really sure what I was doing, but David's confidence provided a sense of safety, which I found extremely comforting. I wrote back with the proposal and posted it off. On the way back from the post box, David asked me if I still had the tape recording equipment I used to use when I interviewed people as a journalist. When we got back to the house, I rummaged round in my desk draws and dug out my trusty old Sony Dictaphone. It was battered and scratched, but it still worked!

David took the small, black machine from me and turned it on.

'Ring me up on the house phone,' he said. 'I want to see how well it records both voices.'

'You don't need to do that. I have a special device that fits into the phone socket on the wall. It records both voices very clearly, and it can't be detected by the other person.' David smiled broadly.

'See – I said you were sneaky!'

It took a while to find the device, which was smaller than a 50 pence piece, and had been stuffed in a box, along with all sorts of miscellaneous electronic bits, when we moved to New Brighton. I plugged it into the phone socket next my desk and connected the tape recorder.

'Phone a friend!' I said to David. He dialled a number and we waited.

'Hello,' said a voice, as the tape recorder automatically turned itself onto record.

'Sorry,' said David. 'Wrong number.' He put the phone down and I pressed reply on the recorder. Both voices came out of the battered little black machine, clear as a bell.

'Gotcha!' said David. 'Right, mate. All we have to do now is wait for the bastard to call us, and we will find out what it is he's got to say for himself. My bet is that he will offer you some cash.'

'What will you say if he does?'

'I don't really know. What do you want me to say?'

I didn't have an answer, but I felt strangely calm about the whole, crazy situation. This was not something I had planned, but, before I could say anything, David put his hand on my shoulder and said 'Don't worry, mate.

Let's just see what he says, and we'll decide what we do next, then.'

Madley had replied to my last letter saying that he would be available to talk to 'Stephen' on Friday, 30 April, at 11:30 am. I had told him that my counsellor was called Stephen as I did not want to disclose David's real name, just in case things got difficult and David lost his temper during the conversation. He had strong feelings about Madley and seemed to hate him with a passion. I would find out why before much longer.

When the time arrived to make the call, I felt physically sick as I turned on the recorder and handed David the phone. He dialled the number and looked at me. I just shrugged. He knew what I meant.

'Hello – is that Hugh? This is Stephen.'

'Hello, yes, it's Hugh here.'

My stomach churned as his voice came through the little monitor on the recorder. I ran to the toilet and vomited.

By the time I had composed myself and sat down once more by the phone, David had stopped speaking. The phone was still pressed tightly to his left ear. He looked pensive and very uncomfortable. He had turned off the monitor so I could not hear what Madley was saying. I leant over to turn it back on, but he stopped me. I sat down again and David put his hand to his mouth, making a vomiting gesture. I didn't really understand what he was trying to say so I looked at him quizzically? David put his hand over the mouthpiece on the phone and whispered to me: 'He's confessing everything that he did to you – he's hysterical.' I looked at him with disbelief.

Twenty minutes later, David ended the conversation, agreeing to call Madley back in fifteen minutes.

'He's says he's wracked with guilt and remorse. He says he wants you to forgive him. He says he'll do anything to help you – I just don't believe him. I think he's playing mind games. He's obviously enjoying telling me what happened'

'Can I listen to the tape?'

'No, not yet. I'm going to call him back. He says he has more to say. It's not very nice – you don't need to hear it now. You know what happened – you were there.'

David's face showed that he had been very distressed by whatever it was Madley had said.

'Did he admit to raping me in the cottage?'

'Yes'

I ran back to the toilet and vomited again.

David called Madley back as arranged and spoke to him for another twenty minutes or so. When it was over, he said we should go for a walk. He wanted to clear his head, and he had something to tell me. We put Timmy on the lead and walked down the hill to the beach. The tide was out so we let Timmy go. He ran like the wind, covering hundreds of yards in seconds. In next to no time, he was a speck on the horizon, and then, just as quickly, he was back with us, soaking wet and loving every minute of it. We walked along the coast line for about an hour, during which time David recounted in his own words what Madley had told him. He was still very upset by what Madley had said. I tried to comfort him by saying that it was O.K., but he was not to be comforted.

'There is something else I need to tell you. It will come as a shock.'

We walked along in silence for a few more minutes. Then David stopped and turned to me. He put his hands on my shoulders to steady me and said. 'They knew all about it – all of them, including the Provincial Rector. Madley told them everything the same night you told him you had spoken to Fr Madden in confession'. I felt my knees start to give way. David held on to me to stop me falling over. My head started to swim and I slumped to the sand. David sat sown next to me as Timmy ran around us, blissfully unaware of the nightmare unfolding within me.

'So that's why they moved him to Battersea then. Not because they didn't believe me, and wanted to protect him from my allegations, but because they knew for sure he was guilty, and they wanted to protect themselves from the scandal.'

'There's more,' said David. 'The Provincial Rector was the same guy who came to interview you in 68. He also interviewed Madley. Madley says he told him everything and was asked to promise that he would never abuse another child. He said on the strength of that promise, the Provincial Rector organised for Madley to be given the job at Battersea, but he was put under close observation for a while by the headmaster at Battersea, who also knew what he had done.'

'What was the Provincial's name?'

'Fr. George Williams, and he's still alive and well.'

'So that means either that their denials to the police were an attempt to pervert justice, or that they kept no records and had no sort of system for tracking known paedophiles. How else can they explain it?'

The magnitude of these revelations took a while to sink in, but the impact of suddenly being told that I had suffered for most of my life, unable to speak out or get justice, when they had known all along that I was telling the truth, was massive. I had to accept the possibility that they had 'forgotten'. How could anyone forget something so serious? Surely it had to be a conspiracy?

'Williams must have banked on the fact that, because they had protected him, Madley would never tell anyone else what had happened. Their secret would be safe as Madley was sure to remain silent. Well now he's done the one thing Williams thought he never would; he's spilt the beans and dobbed them all in! I will make them pay a high price for their treachery.'

A strange sense of calm began to settle on me. I got up and walked over to Timmy, clipped the lead to his collar and said to David: 'Come on, mate. Let's all go home. We have work to do.'

Chapter 17

Gotcha!

When we got back to the house, David told me that Madley had asked if he could speak to him again in a few days, as he wanted to tell him in more detail who knew what, and what had happened when he was interviewed by the Provincial Rector.

'Let's not wait for that. I want to call the police now and tell them what has happened.'

David agreed and poured us both a large glass of red wine while I called Surrey police's head office in Guildford. They put me through to an officer in their vulnerable persons unit at Woking. I explained how we had got to this point and said we had recorded Madley's 'confession'.

'Right', he said, after asking me if David had encouraged Madley in any way during the conversation. I told him that Madley had done almost all of the talking throughout the conversation, and that he had even asked to talk to David again.

'O.K. I'll need to talk to my boss, but someone will come up and see you as soon as I can arrange it. What ever you do, don't lose that tape!'

Half an hour later, the officer rang back to say that he had spoken to his Chief Inspector and to the CPS. They had agreed between them that this was no longer a private criminal prosecution. They would need to launch a complete new investigation!

'Result!' I said to David, as I put the phone down.

'I think we have just pressed the panic button – they are taking over the case!' We finished the wine and opened another bottle!

On 5 May, Madley phoned again to speak to 'Stephen.' This time, we had set up a two-way tape recorder that we had purchased in Liverpool at a specialist hi-fi shop. The machine took ordinary cassettes rather than the mini cassettes my Dictaphone used, making it much easier to transcribe the conversations afterwards.

Both David and I were better prepared this time. I had written down a list of questions to which only Madley could have known the answers. David had learnt the list off by heart until he could ask the questions in a conversational way, as if he were thinking them up as he went rather than reading them. I was desperate to know more detail about who knew what had happened, and how they had conspired to cover it up, but I knew that if we probed Madley too hard, he might clam up – especially if he thought we were recording the conversations.

The key to unlocking his secrets was to keep repeating how much it was helping me to learn more about what had happened. Madley was particularly amazed that no one had told me that he too had confessed to the Salesians following my confession. The thought that I had lived my life thus far under a cloud of suspicion because I thought they had not believed me seemed to disturb him a lot, which gave us a significant advantage that we exploited as best we could.

Over the next couple of days, Madley wrote again, pleading for forgiveness and laying out on paper most of what he had said in the second phone conversation. Reading the material over and over, I began to realise, finally, that I had enough evidence now to put Madley in front of a judge and jury. The shift of power was very healing and it gave me back much of the inner confidence I had lost as a child. I did reply, saying that I had forgiven him, but there were still many more questions to be answered, such as why me?

On the morning of Friday 7 May, a knock at the door brought a serious and much needed dose of reality to the whole crazy episode. Detective Constables Hobbs and Gray introduced themselves and entered the house in a hurry. They had just driven up from Woking, and were both desperate for a pee!

Three hours later, they had completed their mission. All of the letters, the tape recordings and the transcripts were neatly tagged in evidence bags, and they had taken comprehensive statements from both David and myself. John Hobbs was a tough looking, straight talking, no-nonsense policeman. He had served in the force for a long time, yet he still loved the job, despite the sometimes harrowing nature of his current role in child protection. Alison, his colleague, was quietly spoken, yet just as dedicated, and much better looking! Between them, they had made me very much at ease. They were not very precise about what would happen next, and told me to try and not worry too much as things would take time to develop. Before leaving, John shook me hard by the hand and looked me straight in the eyes as he did so.

'We will not fail you Graham,' he said. 'I can promise you that. You will need to be patient though. This is a historical abuse investigation, and they have to take their turn. The higher priority cases, where young children are at risk, have to take precedence. We will get to you eventually, but I can't say exactly when.'

I felt the child in me wanting to say 'No – now, it must be now,' but I managed to keep my composure as I could see in their faces that they knew exactly how I was feeling.

'That's O.K.,' I said. ' I fully understand. After all, what's another few months after all this time?'

My daughter Eve, who had asked if she could sit in during the interview, was also visibly moved by what she had heard. She had wanted the experience as she was about to begin a law degree at Keele University, and she thought the chance to witness a live police interview was too good an opportunity to miss, even though she knew it would be difficult.

After they had gone, I went for a long walk with David and Timmy, while Eve went shopping to clear her mind of the awful things she had just listened to. I did not know at the time, but it was this interview that made her decide later to specialise in child abuse law during her time at University. It seems there is a benefit to everything if you just give things enough time to develop.

The next five months went by surprisingly quickly. My first attempt to tell my story was finally published on 1 September. Called 'Survivor', it had taken me almost two years to find a publisher willing to commit themselves to the project; the majority I had written to – 148 publishers in all – saying it was 'not for them.' Almost all of the rejection slips were very polite and wished me well with the project, but the one that really stood out was the reply from, the good old Catholic Truth Society, who said: 'Thank you for your manuscript, which is well written. Sadly, however, we have concluded that it would not sit comfortably on our list.' I kept them all, but that one I framed and hung on my study wall!

It was, in fact, the Methodists who had the courage to publish my book. They wanted to show their commitment to child protection, and felt it would be one way to demonstrate that they meant what they said. I had to agree to many changes to the manuscript before they made their final decision, which was hard at first, but in the end I knew in my heart that it was better to let the story be told rather than have it sitting in a box under my desk, gathering dust.

Their primary concern, understandably given the effort all the churches were making to protect children, was that they did not want to be seen to be having a dig at the Roman Catholic Church, even if their hand wringing was in reality a case of sealing up the cave door after the dragons had flown. The changes they made to the text were significant, but the end product was still a very harrowing story that pulled no punches, even if all the names were changed, and all references to the Roman Catholicism were removed. Priests became plain 'teachers', and, of course, the ending was not really a satisfactory one. How could it have been – I did not know the full truth of what had happened? The Salesians told me in 2001, during the mediation, that they took a very strong view about such matters now, and they would never cover up child abuse in order to save face or ward off public disgrace. Yet that is exactly what I felt they were still doing, as I had at last found out when Madley finally confessed his guilt to David.

On a bright Sunday morning in October, three days before my birthday, the phone rang in my study.

'Hello Graham – John Hobbs here, mate. Have you got a minute?'

'Yes, of course, what's up?'

'Just to let you know that I arrested Madley early this morning – and guess what?'

'He denied it all again?'

'No, mate. He coughed the lot! He's rolled over Graham. It's all over bar the shouting!'

I was so stunned I just did not know what to say. After a short pause, John told me that he would ring me again later when I'd got over the shock, and let me know some of the details of what Madley had told him. I mumbled a sort of thanks, and he was gone. The tears came fast and furious. Was it really over? Could this be the end of the nightmare? I ran round the house shouting the news to everyone. Barbara cried too, holding me tight as we danced around the kitchen together. This was as much her victory as it was mine. She had put up with my depression for so long now that I knew she had long since stopped believing that I would ever get justice. Well, now things looked very different. I felt such a huge sense of relief, not just for me, but for everyone involved, except Madley, of course – he could burn in hell as far as I was concerned, and all those bastard priests along with him!

Madley was interviewed twice more over the next few days, each time under caution, and each time, refusing to have a solicitor present, a situation that would present a problem later on in the process, but it was still early days as far as the legal machine was concerned. The law is a very slow train.

After the interviews, John Hobbs concluded that he had enough information to send a file to the CPS, and this time, he would make sure that they made 'the right decision'. Sure enough, six weeks later, they charged Madley under the 1963 Sexual Offences Act with three specimen charges, two of indecency with a minor, and one of buggery with a minor, the latter charge carrying a life sentence if convicted.

Events moved fairly swiftly for a while after that. Madley appeared before Woking Magistrates on 22 December, and again on 6 January 2005 before Guildford Crown Court, both appearances being formalities that were over in a few minutes, with no plea being sought at either. Madley would not appear in court again until 3 March, but when he did, along with the judge, the barristers and the court reporters, there would also be two other people sitting in that courtroom. One was me; the other was a miracle, as you shall see.

Chapter 18

Snow-Covered Rainbows

In the weeks that followed Madley's arrest, the nightmares returned. They were always violent, following the same theme each time. I would find myself confronted by men I did not know, usually at a railway station. They would chase me until I was cornered and had only one escape – I would jump onto the track to get away. But then the train would come and bang; it was all over. It was at Mill Hill East tube station, at the top of the Northern Line in North London, that Madley had said to me he would kill himself if I ever told anyone what he was doing to me, and that he would ensure that I would be blamed for his suicide. I can still feel the terror that he instilled into me on that day. I can see his face – that smirk and the contempt in his voice – as he exercised his total control over me.

Not all of the nightmares had the same outcome, however. On a number of occasions, two figures would appear in the distance, walking towards me. As they got closer, I could see that they were calling to me, but I could not hear what they were saying. It was Martin and Nicky, and I tried to shout to them to tell them I couldn't hear what they were saying, but no words came out of my mouth. The silence that had trapped me before was still stopping me now, even in my dreams. I became so distressed during these dreams that I would wake up bathed in sweat, my pillow soaking wet and my heart pounding so loudly I thought it would wake Barbara lying next to me, sleeping peacefully. Oh how I longed for such peaceful sleep.

It was after one more of these dreams that I woke up in a highly disturbed state, shaking and sweating profusely. I was in an almost blind panic and tried to comfort myself by watching the shadows on the wall as they danced together. They were made by the light from the orange street lamp outside our bedroom window, as it filtered through the branches of the sparrow tree that swayed in the breeze blowing in from the sea. As I watched, two figures appeared, then three. They danced together for a moment; an image of happier times, and then they were gone.

'That's it!' I thought to myself. 'I must find Nicky and tell her what happened. I will not be free until she knows.'

I lay there thinking how on earth was I going to find her after all this time? It was thirty-three years since I had last seen her. What if she had gone abroad? What if she was dead? No, she is not dead. That is what Martin is telling me in those dreams. He wants me to tell her to square the circle, to bring us back together once more. The bond between us is still there. Madley may have destroyed me, but he did not destroy the wonderful childhood friendship we had formed. I could feel the energy flowing through me, as I thought about what it would be like to see her again and tell her what had happened all those years ago.

I got up before dawn broke and went down to my study, turned on the computer and ran a 'google' search, firstly for people tracking agencies, then national archives and, finally, Roman Catholic schools in Kent. I knew Nicky had gone to school in Kent, but I could not for the life of me remember the name of her school. Nor could I remember her married name, memories I must have blanked out in the years that followed our separation.

Despite all my efforts, 'no results for your search' kept appearing on the screen. I went and poured myself some coffee and went out into the garden. The moon was still shining brightly in the sky, and the wind was dropping. It was very cold, but somehow I felt a sense of calm. All was not lost. I would just have to try harder to remember something about her that would prove the key to finding her. I would not give up.

I came back in and went into the shower room. Then I saw it, sitting on the towel chest, a copy of the Independent Sunday Review. It was dated 3 October 2004, and written across the cover in large letters was a single sentence: 'The mystery of the Mayfield murder.' It jumped out at me like a cobra.

'Mayfield Girls School; that's where she went. I can find her now!'

I ran back into the study and punched in the name. Seconds later, there it was – the school web site. I searched the past pupils list, but she was not there. Ah, well – some times they don't include everyone, I thought. At the bottom of the page was a list of contacts, one of which was the editor of the school magazine. I sent her an e-mail saying that I was trying to find Veronica Allen, but I had lost touch with her years ago, and wondered if she had a contact address for the magazine?

It was not until later in the day that I received her reply. Yes, she did
have a married name and current address, in England, but she could
not give it to me without permission. 'If you would like to send a letter
to Veronica, at the school address, I will forward it onto her.' I was so
excited that I could hardly contain myself. I poured some more coffee and
began to write my letter. It was not as difficult as I had thought it would
be, almost writing itself as it went along. I apologised for bringing such
difficult news, but explained that there might soon be a trial, which she
might hear about, so I wanted her to hear about it from me, rather than
read about it in the media. I told her that I still thought about her and
her parents a great deal, and I hoped she and they were well, although
in my heart I had a sad feeling that her parents might not still be alive. I
signed my letter 'Bim', the childhood name by which she had known me,
enclosed a copy of my book, sealed up the package and walked down to
the post office with Timmy.

A week went by, and then, one morning, a message appeared in my
e-mail. 'A note from Nicky' said the subject line. I opened it up nervously, and read the words on the screen. It only took a second to realise
that I had found my salvation – she was alive and well, and so glad that
I had told her. 'I am still reeling from the truth. There is so much to tell
you, some sad, some very happy. Please call me when you can. Here is
my number. I just can't believe it.'

I picked up the phone and began to dial her number. My hand shook as
I pressed the keys. I thought of everything I wanted to say, but my mind
went blank as the ringing tones began. Any second now and I would hear
her voice again. My heart felt as if it was about to explode.

'Hello?'

'Hello Nicky; it's me.'

'Bim!'

I tried to speak but the words would not come out.

'Bim? Are you there?'

I took a deep breath and began to talk. The tears rolled down my face
as I started, nervously, to say some of the things I wanted to tell her. She
listened carefully, asking questions when I paused, and then, as if a magic
wand had been waved, the conversation became much less difficult, even
when she talked about the death of her parents and her eldest sister, Helen.
The sadness she felt was reflected in her voice, but she knew I wanted to
know everything that had happened, as I had known and loved them all.
The more we talked, the further the years rolled back until we had covered
everything of note that had happened since we had last spoken.

After about an hour, I said that there was still a bit more to be said
about what had happened to me, but it would be much easier to talk face

to face. At the end of the conversation we agreed that we should go and visit Martin's grave together, and perhaps there we would be able to lay the past to rest once and for all. There was no need to be sad anymore. We said goodbye and I put the phone back in its cradle. I felt such a surge of joy flowing through me. At last I could see the light at the end of the tunnel, and this time, it would not fade, as it had done so many times before.

On 22 November, I left before dawn broke and drove to Reading, arriving at 7 am; far too early to call, so I sat in the car not far from Nicky's house and waited. It was almost surreal. There in front of me, maybe not more than 100 yards away, was the house in which lived the only person on the planet who could really set me free. All she had to do was tell me that she understood, but as I sat there, wondering what it would be like to see her again, the doubts grew in my mind. Would she even recognise me after all this time? Would she still like me, or would she be distant because of what I had told her? Then, after half an hour, I could wait not a second longer. I had to see her face again. I knew in my heart that as soon as I looked into her eyes, I would know the answer. I started the car and drove quietly up to the house and stopped by the gate, at which point the front door opened and there she was.

Nicky walked to the car and got in beside me.

'Hello Bim. It's so good to see you again. It's been such a long time.'

Thirty-three years, two months and four days to be precise!

We were both lost for words, but after looking at each other in silence for a few moments, she said 'Come on; park the car and we'll go and have some coffee. I have still got so much to tell you.' My fears began to melt away as I realised that she was not in any way disgusted by what I had told her, in fact she made a point of talking about everything else but what had happened. We would face that when we went to see Martin's grave later that morning.

As midday approached, Nicky said we should go now and do what we had to do. I was feeling very uncomfortable inside. I knew I would cry, but I did not want to make too much of a fuss.

'I've got some tissues,' Nicky said, with a familiar kindness in her voice. I could hear her mother in those words. She looked nervous too, but she had a purpose about her. It would be all right.

On the way to the cemetery, we stopped outside her old family house in New Malden, where we had spent so many happy hours as young teenagers. It brought back great waves of emotion, and I could not hold back the tears. Nicky leaned over and wiped my eyes with her fingers.

'Come on, we will finish this together.'

It took us a while to find Martin's grave, but when we did, all my fears began to dissolve. There, next to him, lay his sister Dilly, his mother, father and grandmother. Almost the entire family at rest together. We touched the grave stones and bowed our heads in silent prayer. After a while, when we had said what we wanted to say to each of them, I looked at Nicky, and saw for the first time the pain she carried inside. She had experienced so much sadness over the years, but yet she was still so brave. In that moment, the years slipped back and we stood there once more as children. I took her hand, pulled her gently towards me and began to cry.

As I held her in my arms, it started to rain, not heavily, but enough to wet our faces. I looked directly into her eyes as my tears mingled with the raindrops.

'I'm sorry I didn't tell you at the time. I was just so scared. I thought I would lose you if I told you what was happening. It was all so difficult – and I lost you anyway.'

'You didn't lose me Bim. I lost you. I just couldn't understand what had gone wrong. I thought you didn't love me anymore. I don't really know what I would have done if you had told me at the time, but I wouldn't have sent you away.'

I started to say something, but Nicky put her fingers to my lips to stop me.

'It's all right Bim. This is where the pain stops. Martin brought us back here so that I could help you put the past to rest forever. He wants you to live in happiness, Bim, for him and Helen and Dilly, and for your children and Barbara. There is so much living still to be done.'

As she spoke, the rain stopped and the sun came out. A large rainbow formed in the sky at the far end of the cemetery, followed moments later by a second.

'Look,' she said. There is the proof that the bond between the three of us never died.'

'I don't understand,' I said, looking towards the sparkling bands of coloured light.

'Well, what we had then, and still have now, is friendship. It is very special; like those beautiful rainbows – they are the love that we all shared together. They just got covered in snow when the coldness froze your life, so you couldn't see them anymore. But they were always there; you just had to wait for the snow to melt.

'I never forgot you, Bim, but we can't turn back the clock, and nor do we need to. Whatever life has in store for us in the future, I can promise you this – I will always be your friend.' She took my hand and we walked slowly out of the cemetery. The long, lonely nightmare was finally over. I was free at last.

Chapter 19

Waiting for Justice. . . .

The miracle sitting next to me in that courtroom in Guildford on 3 March 2005 was, of course, Nicky. Barbara had desperately wanted to be there too, but she had an important school event to attend, and we had both agreed that the children should come first. They would have been so disappointed had she not been there, so I asked Nicky if she would come with me, as I knew I would need someone I could trust to support me. It would be the first time she had ever seen the man who had caused so much heartache, and it would be the first time I had seen him since I had left school all those years ago.

I drove down to Guildford the evening before, and stayed with my elder sister, Sharron. It was good to see her again, and she helped me keep focused on what was really important – family and friends. The following day, I got up before dawn and went for a walk. The air was cold and the night's frost sparkled in the moonlight. Everything was so still; it was as if time itself had been put on hold for me while I prepared to face my nemesis. As the first signs of dawn began to brighten the sky, I walked back to the house. Sharron was sitting at the kitchen table drinking a cup of tea. She had made me some breakfast, but I could not eat. We chatted for a while, then, I kissed her on the forehead and said it was time to go.

'Take care, my little brother. You will win in the end.'

Nicky lived about thirty minutes drive away, not far in a warm car, but my heater had given up the ghost on the drive down from Liverpool, and it was still below freezing outside. When I knocked on her front door, I was so cold my fingers had gone numb.

It had only been four months since I had last stood here, but it felt much longer. The door opened and there she stood; wet hair, no make up; my guardian angel.

'Sorry it's so early. I couldn't sleep!'

'Neither could I. Come in and have some coffee while I get ready – you look frozen.'

We got to the court in plenty of time. I have always had a thing about being on time. It goes back to the fear the Salesians put into us if you were ever late for school. We were both feeling very uncomfortable, feelings which grew worse as we waited and waited in the corridor outside court No 3, while the defence barrister talked behind closed doors with the prosecution barrister, emerging after some two hours to scurry off into yet more discussions. Nicky began to shows signs of distress, but she was trying so hard not to let me notice.

'Don't worry Nicky – he looks a lot more troubled than we feel!'

'Have you seen him?'

'Yes – look down the far end of the corridor, behind that glass partition. That's him with his solicitor.'

'Are you sure?'

'Believe me; that's him.'

The grey-haired old man sitting behind the glass wall was looking at us. He knew it was me, and I knew it was him. The man who had stolen my childhood and wrecked so much of my life was now about to answer for his actions. I felt very confused. There was no sense of triumph, just a burning desire to run away, as far from here as I could get.

Nicky could sense it.

'Look at me, not him. He is all on his own, but you are not – not anymore. He may have pulled us apart, but he didn't win did he? We are still here, and now it's his turn to be frightened.'

'Hello Graham!' said a familiar voice behind me. I turned and smiled as I looked at the immaculately dressed figure of D.C. John Hobbs.

'Well, bless me. You scrub up well!'

'Cheeky git,' he said with a broad grin, which put me at ease in an instant.

'This is Nicky.'

'I though it might be. Hello, Nicky. Good of you to come here. I know it must be difficult for you, but we should be in court soon. The barrister wants to see us for a moment. It's not what we'd hoped for, but it's what we had expected.'

My heart sank as John led us into a small briefing room. The barrister and a couple of other suits were waiting for us in the room. They did not look too happy.

'I'll come straight out with it,' said the barrister – who reminded me of my daughter Eve, and was not much older!

'Madley's defence team has thrown in an abuse of process argument, which they want to put before the judge. That means Madley will not be pleading guilty today. The best we can hope for is that the judge will still arraign him today, but it will mean we will be coming back at some time in the future to hear their argument.'

I was lost for words.

'Is he going to walk?' asked Nicky.

'No,' said the barrister. 'I'm afraid that the only defence they have is to try and have the evidence that we have thrown out of court. They have the right to try, but don't worry. They will face a hard fight. We have a very strong case. It's not going to be easy for them at all.'

The court PA system burst into life.

'All parties in the Madley case to court 3 please.'

My heart began to race. I reached for Nicky's hand and held it tightly as we followed the suits into the court.

John led us to the public gallery, just a few feet away from the dock, in which sat Madley behind a glass panel. He looked nervous and his hands were trembling as he listened to the clerk read out the charges.

Even though Nicky knew what the charges were, hearing them spoken in such detail in the formality of the courtroom, in front of all these people, made her wince. She looked at me with real anger in her eyes, and whispered: 'how could he have done that to you? Such a wicked man.'

Before I could answer, the clerk asked him in a stern voice: 'how do you plead – guilty or not guilty?'

Madley hesitated for a moment, then said in a faltering voice: 'not guilty.'

Nicky leaned into me to stop me from standing up. She knew I was about to jump up and shout 'LIAR!'

I felt sick, but the judge's voice brought me back under control.

'I am prepared to hear your abuse argument at the next convenient date, but I want him arraigned for trial now. I don't want any further delays – it's already taken much too long.'

John looked at me and put his thumb up. The clerk gave out a date for the next hearing, and then it was all over. My head was still swimming as I stood up to leave, only to be pulled back down into my seat. I had not even seen Madley step down from the dock, but Nicky had. Her swift intervention had stopped me from bumping into him as he filed passed me and hurried out of the court.

John came over and told us to wait in the court for a moment, just to give Madley time to leave the building. My head was spinning. I wanted to get out into the fresh air as fast as possible. John could see how distressed I was, so he took me by the arm and led the way. We must have looked like a row of ducks as I was still clutching Nicky's hand tightly as the three of us filed out of the court room.

Once outside, I soon recovered, but Nicky's face was ashen. She was shaking and close to tears. John took hold of her and whispered something to her that I could not hear. She looked up at him and smiled.

'Come on you,' she said, taking me once more by the hand. 'Let's get out of this place.'

I shook John's hand and thanked him for everything he had done.

'It'll be O.K. We will get him in the end. You'll see.'

We said our farewells, and went our separate ways. I knew it would be months before we would meet again, the judicial system being no friend of the victim when it comes to the length of time it takes for 'due process' to shuffle along at its glacial pace. By now, however, I had learnt to be patient. I just hoped and prayed that the outcome would be worth the wait.

As the weeks rolled by, I put my efforts into challenging the Salesians once more, only, this time, the boot was on the other foot. Madley's confession to the police had blown their cover, but, as my mother kept reminding me: 'they are the third largest religious order in the world. They have so much power – I fear for your safety.'

I know that she meant well, but such warnings of impending doom were not what I needed, nor did they make me feel that either of my parents had really understood what had happened. My mother, in particular, was still mired in the belief that child abuse was all about men in dirty raincoats, not something her beloved church would possibly be involved in.

It was pointless for me to try and change her belief system. Years of brainwashing and indoctrination had done its work. As long as she still derived some comfort from her faith, then who was I to put doubt in her mind? My battle was with the Salesians, not with my mother, so I wrote to my old headmaster, Fr O'Shea, asking him to explain why, in the light of what we now knew, he had told the police back in April 2000 that he simply could not recall any event involving me. He did not reply himself, but sent a message via Fr Bailey, one of the two priests who represented the Salesians at the mediation. The message politely but firmly instructed me not to contact Fr O'Shea again as my letter had 'upset him.'

So, then, the once all-powerful priest who had beaten me severely with a wooden stick when I was a child – punishment for accidentally breaking a milk bottle at lunch-time in the school refectory – could not even find the courage to respond to me in person now that he had been found out. How I hated these priests, but hatred would not bring me any closer to the truth, so I wrote to the current Provincial Rector, Fr Peter Preston, and challenged him once more to deny that they had no knowledge of what had happened to me. I also asked him to apologise to me, something they had so far refused absolutely to do. His reply; short and to the point, simply said: 'This matter is now in the hands of our lawyers. I can make no further comment.'

So, despite all of hand-wringing they had done at the mediation in February 2001, trumpeting their adherence to the recommendations that followed Lord Nolan's inquiry into child abuse in the Roman Catholic Church in England and Wales, whose central theme was that every case of suspected child abuse, whenever it might have occurred, should be investigated, they were still unwilling to tell the truth and face the consequences. Such was their institutional arrogance, reinforced in a letter from their lawyers, which arrived a week later, threatening me with an injunction if I made any attempt to re-open my case against them.

The Salesians' own child protection policy, which they had also proudly waved in front of me at the mediation, stated that they would investigate every reported case of child abuse within their schools, regardless of how embarrassing such an investigation might be. My sense of anger over their continued denials was, therefore, difficult to overcome. I passed their letter to Stephen Wilde, and asked him to respond robustly, which he did in his customary way; polite, but with as much contempt in his tone as he could muster – the professional rules of engagement between lawyers allowing!

'I am advised that, should you do that, my client will happily defend such an action in the High Court, and then everything you are trying to keep quiet would come into the public domain anyway. I suggest you ask your client to consider the matter a little further.' They did, and we heard no more from them!

At the same time, I also wrote to the Secretary of State for Education once more, asking him why it was that, despite all the Nolan recommendations , the Salesians, which although private was, after all, a state aided organisation, still felt able to deny their involvement in covering up my case? Where were the checks and balances that were supposed to be in place now to ensure that Roman Catholic schools did not use their power to hide behind their black cloaks of silence and secretiveness? How could a state-aided school, funded from the public purse, still be outside the rules that governed other schools on child protection? I got no response.

It was not until July 2005 that David and I received the formal notification from the CPS, instructing us to attend court as witnesses at a pre-trial hearing, to be held sometime in August, the exact date of which we would be advised of, with only 24 hours notice! At last, things were beginning to move again, but, as the weeks rolled by, David began to show the all too familiar signs of a deepening depression. I knew the symptoms so well: mood swings, loss of interest, sadness, unexplained tears. At first, my brave marine refused to listen, when I urged him to go and see Dr Price, who worked closely with the charity we ran, and knew us both very well.

'I'm fine – stop worrying,' he would say, but I had come to know this man well by now and I knew in my heart that he was struggling. Now it was my turn to look after him.

Eventually, David went to see Dr Price, who confirmed my suspicion that he was suffering from post-traumatic stress disorder. What neither of us knew was the exact cause of David's problems, although he had told both of us something of the abuse he had suffered as a child, he had not been able to disclose the whole story. What was nagging at the back of my mind now was, had what he had been exposed to by me been the trigger that re-opened his abuse memories? I asked David directly if that was the case. He tried to dismiss the question so as not to cause me concern, but I knew that what Madley had told him about me had really effected him, and I felt a terrible sense of guilt beginning to grow within me.

I called Peter Green, who had been so supportive to me during my earlier battle with the Salesians, and dumped my worries on him.

'I'm not surprised,' he said. 'Given David's military history, his problems will be much more complicated to resolve. I suggest you put him touch with Nick Cooling. If he can't sort him out, no-one can.'

Nick Cooling is one of, if not the, best psychiatrists in the UK, specialising in sexual abuse and other forms of serious trauma. He has a practice in Huddersfield, but spends much of his time working at the Priory Hospital in Roehampton, famous for its celebrity clients, so you can imagine his fees! Fortunately, David had an insurance policy that covered mental-health problems, so, after an initial assessment, Dr Cooling admitted him to the Priory, where he underwent intensive psychotherapy for three weeks, at the end of which, David emerged, less tormented than when he had gone in, but still deeply troubled. I was at least able to take some comfort from his assurance that, while the events of the past year had re-opened his own nightmare; our shared experience had provided him with a gateway through which he could finally begin to heal his wounds. I made him a promise that, what ever happened from now on, I would always be there by his side.

Chapter 20

Test of Courage

On Monday, 1 August, 2005, John Hobbs phoned me with the news we had all been waiting for.

'Steel yourself, mate. Your day in court has finally arrived – it's Wednesday. The defence has put up what we call a 'kitchen sink' argument. They are going to try and get the judge to throw out all of the evidence we have on the basis that we screwed up the interview process. It's bollocks, Graham, but they will do their level best to discredit you, and me, but particularly you.'

'How will they come at me?

'They will say you were gathering evidence; that you are a liar; only after money.'

'But the agreement I signed with the Salesians prevents me from suing Madley?'

'I know, mate. That's our trump card – they don't know about the agreement. Bring it with you, and try not to worry. We have come this far, and our barrister will fight them every inch of the way. Get yourself down here safely, and I'll see you bright and early at court on Wednesday morning.'

The next two days seemed like eternity as I watched the clock tick by. I gathered together all of the hundreds of documents about my case I had amassed over the past five years, not that I thought I would need them, but just in case, and packed my bag. John had said the court hearing was listed for two days. It was going to be a fight, but I was up for a fight. If they really thought they could crush my spirit, they had not listened to the voice of the child within me. It would not just be me in that court; it would be the child they tried to destroy as well. I would not let his voice be silenced. I would look the beast squarely in the eye and tell my story – after all, I had nothing to lose anymore. I was at peace; the truth had set me free.

David and I drove down to Guildford on Tuesday afternoon; trusting our journey to public transport having been ruled out by the on-going chaos wrought by the London bombings on 7 July. We spent the evening with Richard, a friend who lived just outside Guildford. He knew something of what was going on, but not all. Many drinks later, with the moon and stars listening thoughtfully above us, as we sat in his back garden, I told him everything that had happened. He had known me as a close friend since childhood; shared a flat with me in London; gone out with my sister; and thought he knew everything about me there was to know. Such is the nature of child abuse. Its legacy of silence crushes its victims with the power and density of a black hole. But unlike the billions of stellar objects trapped in a black hole, my silence was about to escape – in a court; in front of a judge; in front of the public.

I woke early, to find David already up and dressed. We made some coffee while Richard slept on, his drinking days evidently behind him.

'Poor lad,' said David. 'These southern Jesses just can't take their booze.'

I reminded him that I was a Southern Jesse too.

'Not any longer, mate. You're an honorary scouser now. You have been pardoned for your home-counties upbringing!' David was trying hard to stop me thinking about what we were about to go through. He was a true rock, and I needed him badly.

'Cometh the hour, cometh the man,' I said, as we parked the car and walked up the court steps. The sun was shining. We were both very nervous, but we were there. I had asked Barbara not to come. There was no need for her to watch me fight my way through this nest of vipers. She had seen me in battle before, and knew it was not a pretty sight, particularly if I lost!

Nicky was on holiday in France with her family, but she had given me her glasses chain to wear, and Philip, her husband, who had been so supportive ever since Nicky had told him about me, had sent me a blue tie. It was his favourite tie, not just because he liked it, but, because he had worn it at his daughter's wedding, and now he wanted me to wear it.

'It's a special tie, Bim,' he had told me. 'It will give you strength, knowing that you are in our thoughts.'

John Hobbs was waiting for us at the top of the steps. His cheery grin was a great comfort.

'Well, mate. This is where we have got to. If we win the legal argument, the judge will allow all the evidence to go forward to trial, and Madley will be well and truly knackered. However; if we lose, then it's all over mate. He will walk. That doesn't mean he has been cleared – but it does mean he won't stand trial.'

John's face told me that he was frustrated to the point of exasperation with the machinations of the legal process.

'It's hard enough trying to catch these bastards,' he said, 'and then you have to go through a bloody assault course, a minefield and God knows what else to try and get a conviction.'

'John, don't beat yourself up, mate,' I said, putting my hand on his broad shoulder. 'You have got me a lot further than I would have got without you. Let's just see what happens. If we lose, then we lose. So what? We tried – but we might win! Let's just get on with it.'

John led the way through security, and then to the witness room. On the way, we passed Madley, sitting alone in the corridor. He stared at me as I walked past him. I looked back at him with as much fury as I could muster.

'I will beat you this time,' I said under my breath. 'Just you wait and see.'

We sat down in the witness room. John shut the door behind us.

'Did you see the state of him?' he said. 'If you put him in a room with 100 other people, and said 'spot the paedophile', you know who they'd point to, don't you?'

We all laughed, but then it was time to be serious. I was called in first. As I took the stand and swore the oath, my voice was strong, but my mouth was as dry as a desert. My hands began to shake as I put my reading glasses on and opened the large file of papers the court clerk had handed me. I adjusted my special tie, took a deep breath and prepared for the worst. I was ready.

Six gruelling hours later, it was all over. I had won, but only just. The defence portrayed me as a liar, saying that I had been underhand and deceitful, entrapping Madley into admitting things during the telephone conversations that he would not have said had he known we were re-cording the phone calls. They said much the same to David, and tried to show the police to have been incompetent in their handling of Madley's interviews. The judge said he was unimpressed with my testimony, and described my police witness statement as being of little worth, but he did not agree that the police interviews with Madley should not be admitted as evidence and refused the defence application that the whole case should be thrown out. He ordered that the tape-recorded phone calls could not be submitted as evidence, but the police interviews could go forward to trial. The letters Madley had written to me were also dismissed as being of no material value.

'Don't be disheartened, Graham,' John said, outside on the court steps.

'We were never going to use the tape recordings or the letters anyway. You should both be very proud of what you have achieved today. Madley's barrister is a very experienced lawyer. He only brought the tapes into the argument to try and destroy your character – but he failed! Well done, both of you. This has been a good day. Get yourselves home now. I'll be in touch.'

I rang Barbara and told her. She was beside herself with joy. This had been as much her trial as mine, yet she was so happy for me. Then I rang Nicky. She was on a riverboat, somewhere in northern France.

'Well, how did it go?'

'Just tell Philip the tie worked!'

There was a scream of delight from the other end, and then my phone went dead, its battery now as exhausted as I was.

David and I climbed into the car, buckled up and headed north. Our job was done here for now, but we would be back.

Chapter 21

Trial – and Error

And so it was, on the morning of 12 December, 2005, David and I walked up the steps of Guildford Crown Court to face my tormentors once more. In the left hand pocket of my jacket, unbeknown to me at the time, a small, white angel nestled. Barbara had placed it there to keep me safe. It had been given to her many years ago by her mother, and she had put it there without telling me, hoping I would find it and realise its significance, which, of course, I did as soon as I emptied my pockets during the security check at the court entrance. 'What's that?' asked David.

'It's a symbol of everything that is good my friend. It is telling me there are powerful forces at work here, not all of which will make any sense for some time to come.'

'You don't half talk some bollocks at times, mate!' he said, as we picked up our possessions from the grubby plastic container the security guard had thrust at us on the other side of the metal detector gate.

Barbara had stayed at home in Liverpool, because we had agreed it would be easier for me to face my ordeal without having to worry about her sitting there and listening to all of the horror that would come out in the trial, as she was still having to deal with the fallout of her own brush with so-called justice, having herself just been through an independent inquiry into allegations of corrupted management practices, racial abuse and bullying at her school, in which she had given evidence as a witness.

Her treatment at the hands of the local authority, which employed her, had been a very bruising experience, virtually destroying her enthusiasm as a teacher, and testing our relationship to its core, as those under investigation had used my problems, which she had told them about in confidence a long time ago, to assassinate her character as a witness. They failed, but the process left her feeling isolated and betrayed, a feeling I knew only too well.

'Hello lads,' said John Hobbs, as he greeted us outside the witness room. 'I think you'll find a bit of a surprise waiting for you in there, Graham!'

The smile on his face reached from ear to ear, as he opened the door for me and directed me in.

'Nicky? I don't believe it. Why didn't you tell me you were coming?'

'Because you would have told me not to! I thought you might need some extra support – so here I am. I'll go if you want me to.'

She looked pensive and anxious, but the smile on her face, whilst not quite as wide as John's, told me that there was no way she was going to leave – regardless of what I said!

'No, please stay. This whole sorry mess began with us, so I guess it should finish with us too.'

John Hobbs looked at David and put his fingers to his mouth in a mock gagging gesture! David burst out laughing, breaking the tension, and we all fell about, much to the obvious disapproval of the usher, who had just come into the room to summon John into the court.

I now had two angels and a burly marine to help me, but even their power could not change what was about to happen.

For the next six hours, the three of us sat patiently outside courtroom number four, as John Hobbs and his colleagues trooped endlessly backwards and forwards between the courtroom and the police room, as the defence counsel called for ever more pieces of paper.

At 4:30 in the afternoon, John emerged from the courtroom, his face by now having lost any hint of humour.

'It's not going well, Graham. The defence are arguing that Madley was mentally ill when he made his statement to me, and he should have been given an appropriate adult to sit with him during the interview. They even produced a fucking expert psychiatrist to prove that he is a nutter!'

'What happens now?' I asked him nervously.

'Well, the judge has listened to it all again, and he says he needs a day to make a decision, but I can tell you, there will not now be a trial. The defence have said they will enter a guilty plea if the judge rules against them and allows the interview to go in as evidence, but if he throws it out – it's all over mate. I suggest you go home and wait for me to call you. I'm sorry Graham. I did all I could, but I did warn you how difficult this might be. It's not about his guilt. I told the judge that he was guilty of these crimes, and no one has said differently. It's all about the legal process – it's stacked so heavily in favour of the defendant in cases like yours.'

John stood up abruptly, shook me warmly by the hand, and hurried away, but not before I had noticed the tiniest hint of moisture in his eyes. This had not been a good day for the police, and he was clearly distressed.

David, Nicky and I looked at each other for a moment and then got up to go without saying anything more. As we made our way down the corridor in silence, we passed Madley and his defence team, huddled together in a corner near the front entrance. I stopped to look at him. He stared at me with a cold, empty expression. It was a look I had seen many times before, but this time it did not fill me with the fear that it had in the past. David and Nicky had also stopped, just a few feet away from me. They walked back to where I stood, looked at Madley, and reached out to take each of my hands in theirs, and stood there either side of me, glaring back at him. It was a far more powerful display of defiance than words alone could have ever created. Madley withered visibly, then turned away and stared at the ground.

We walked away, still in silence.

'So, who is really the winner here, Bim,' asked David, 'you or him?'

'I don't feel like a winner at the moment, but you are right. Whatever the judge decides, everyone now knows the truth. I did what I could, and that's all that matters. Let's get out of here before I thump him!'

We left the court and made our way to the car park. On the windscreen of our car, a bright yellow parking ticket proudly announced that we were ten minutes over time, and now owed the local authority £30!

David ripped the ticket from the glass and stuffed it into my pocket.

'There you go, mate. Compliments of the great British judicial system!'

We said goodbye to Nicky and headed north once more. I had a strong sense that it would be a while before I saw her again, but yet there was no sadness in this goodbye. Seeing her again had finally buried the doubts I had had about the value of friendship. I will always love her, but through my ordeal I have come to understand that there are some things in life that you just can't have, but if you fret about that too much, you lose sight of those things that you do have, friendship being by far the most important. I have met many people in this world who appear to have everything, but in reality, have nothing as they have never experienced true friendship, a gift that demands nothing, but gives everything. I have Barbara, David, my three wonderful children and now Nicky, and they are all true friends. Madley, on the other hand, has no-one. A lonely, miserable little man, whose only claim to fame must be that, albeit unwittingly, he created in me a determination to stand up and be a strong voice for those who are still silent. That is my destiny and nothing he, nor the Salesians, nor the Roman Catholic Church, nor anyone else for that matter, can stop me fulfilling.

Two days later, on Friday morning, 16 December, David and I were sitting in my study, waiting for the phone to ring. Barbara had just brought in some coffee when the call came through. I put the phone on loudspeaker. John's subdued voice filled the room – it was over – we had lost the battle. Madley had been set free by the judge – not declared innocent, but not found guilty either.

'It all came down to a tick in the wrong box, Graham. The custody sergeant had ticked the box that said Madley had asked for a responsible adult to be present. He should have ticked the box next to it that said he had refused our offer, because that's what really happened, Graham. Madley's defence said that he had asked for a responsible adult, but he didn't. That tick in the wrong box – an honest mistake – was sufficient to sway the judge that there was some doubt, and, because of that doubt, he could not let my interview go forward to a trial. I'm sorry, mate. I know how much this will hurt you after everything you've been through. If it's any consolation to you, the CPS have said you should sue him in a civil court, where the burden of proof is on the balance of probability, and not beyond reasonable doubt, as it is in a criminal trial. I will be more than happy to be a witness for you.'

At first I was lost for words, but I could see the sense of relief on Barbara's face. She did not say anything, but I knew what she was thinking. It was time to draw a line in the sand and move on. Life is too short to keep raking over the coals of disaster.

'No thanks John. I appreciate the offer, but I owe to my family to stay away from the law courts for now – the emotional cost on everyone has been far too high – but there's still the court of public opinion to go to, and that's where I'm going next.'

'What do you mean, Graham?'

'I'm a writer, John – you'll see!'

Chapter 22

Child Abuse – The Hidden Cost

When Lord Filkin wrote to me, in his capacity as Minister of State for Education, his decision not to open an investigation into my case, based on the notion that Lord Nolan's investigation into abuse in the Roman Catholic Church in England and Wales had already resolved the problems of child abuse in the Roman Catholic Church, he failed not just me, but every other child in our so-called civilised nation, by refusing to face the stark reality of the hidden cost of child abuse in society as a whole.

In April 2003, when David and I set up the Lantern Project, we knew that there was a desperate lack of understanding of the true impact child abuse has on individuals, and very poor provision to deal with the problems it causes, but the scale of the problem only began to emerge as the numbers of victims asking for our help began to grow.

By January 2006, our website (www.survivorslantern.org) had received close to one million hits from 90,000 individuals, all of whom told virtually the same story. No one wanted to listen to them, and their lives continued to be plagued by the profound impact their experiences had had on them. The vast majority of them said that they found it almost impossible to seek help, and when those brave enough to ask for help had done so, they were shut down, ignored, often vilified, and always left feeling worse than before they had disclosed their stories.

As word of the project spread, we began to receive referrals from the prison service, the probation service, psychiatric units, GP practices, women's refuges and numerous other charitable groups working with vulnerable children and adults. The more we talked to these people, the more we began to understand the true cost of child abuse in our society.

Almost 80% of the men and women in prison we talked to, told the same story. They had been abused as children, and found life impossible to cope with, leading them to seek refuge in drug and alcohol abuse, petty crime, violence, self harm and progressively more serious offending behaviour, until, finally, they ended up in prison.

The victims we talked to who had not become involved in offending behaviour, had a similar story, except that they had ended up, not in a prison with walls, but in a prison of the mind, often with long histories of mental health problems, self harm, debt, broken relationships and loneliness. The only victims we could not talk to, were those for whom these problems had proved too much, taking their own lives in one last, desperate attempt to rid themselves of the horrors of their past.

The professionals we talked to gave us the harsh facts, as they are currently understood. One out of every four children in the UK has been abused, 38% of girls are sexually abused before the age of 18, 16% of boys are sexually abused before the age of 18 and between 90% and 95% of all sexual abuse cases go unreported to the police because the victims fear they will not be believed. The police told us that of the cases that are reported to them, only 2% end in a successful prosecution – and even then, the sentences handed down by the courts are often so short that the perpetrators are freed within a matter of a few months, the majority going on to commit further offences against children.

Dr Nick Cooling, one the UK's leading psychiatrists, specialising in sexual abuse trauma, told us that if you took a typical street, anywhere in the country, you will find sexual abuse occurring in every fifth house, and one or more of the other forms of child abuse (neglect, emotional abuse and physical abuse) occurring in every third house, yet, child abuse is not talked about. From time to time, the tabloid press get on their high horse and mount a campaign against particular individuals who have murdered the children they abused. Ian Brady, Roy Whiting, Ian Huntley, to name but three 'trophy cases', as the tabloids call them.

But, as a nation, we are still not ready, or even willing, to face the fact that so much of the anti-social behaviour, drug abuse, petty crime, suicide and general misery that occurs in our country has its roots in the millions of young children that suffer sexual abuse on a daily basis, most of which goes unnoticed and unchallenged.

As my case shows only too clearly, finding the courage to disclose what has happened, and then trying do something about it, is such a huge and complex task, when faced with the wall of institutional silence that stands in your way, and the brutality of a system of justice that is outdated, incompetent, self serving, for those who make their living out of it, and designed primarily to protect the defendant, not the victim.

My book is not likely to set the oceans on fire, nor will it put right the wrongs of the past, nor stop the abuse that will occur tomorrow, and the day after, and the day after. But it might just help others find the way out of their darkness and find the support that they need to climb the long ladder that takes you from the pit of despair back into the sunshine.

From all that I have been through, I have this message for my fellow survivors: Be proud of who you are. You are unique and wonderful individuals, something you can and should celebrate. You are not alone, and you will survive if you want to, but you really have to want to. Don't be afraid to ask for help, but don't expect the world to stop and listen to you when you do. Ours is a tiny voice in a very violent storm, but if we all shout together, someone will eventually hear us.

Graham Wilmer's story, told here, is based on a large body of written material. Many of the letters, court and police documents, can be found at his website: www.grahamwilmer.org.uk.

Graham's charity, the Lantern Project, supporting those who have been abused as children, can be found at: www.survivorslantern.org.